FAST AND SLOW PITCH

BY
MARIO PAGNONI
and
GERALD ROBINSON

The Athletic Institute
North Palm Beach, FL 33480

Copyright © 1990 by Mario Pagnoni and Gerald Robinson
and The Athletic Institute
Photographs © 1990 Mountain Lion, Inc.
Photographs on pages 45, 46, 58, 67, 68, 103, 104, 128,
129, 145, 153, 172, 182, 184 193, 194, 204, and 206
© 1990 John Mottern

All rights reserved
including the right of reproduction
in whole or in part in any form
Published by The Athletic Institute
200 Castlewood Drive
North Palm Beach, Florida 33408
Printed in the United States of America

Library of Congress Catalog Card Number 89-82614
ISBN 0-87670-150-0

A Word from the Publisher

This Sports Publication is but one item in a comprehensive list of sports instructional aids, such as video cassettes and 16 mm films, which are made available by The Athletic Institute. This book is part of a master plan which seeks to make the benefits of athletics, physical educational and recreation available to everyone. To obtain a free catalog, please write to the Athletic Institute at the address listed on the copyright page.

The Athletic Institute is a not-for-profit organization devoted to the advancement of athletics, physical education and recreation. The Institute believes that participation in athletics and recreation has benefits of inestimable value to the individual and to the community.

The nature and scope of the many Institute programs are determined by a Professional Advisory Committee, whose members are noted for their outstanding knowledge, experience and ability in the fields of athletics, physical education and recreation.

The Institute believes that through this book the reader will become a better performer, skilled in the fundamentals of this fine event. Knowledge and the practice necessary to mold knowledge into playing ability are the keys to real enjoyment in playing any game or sport.

John D. Riddle
President and Chief Executive Officer
The Athletic Institute

James Hotchkiss
Executive Director
The Athletic Institute

Table of Contents

Note: When practicing or playing softball, be certain to use the proper equipment, including appropriate protective headgear when batting and protective masks, chest and shin guards when catching. Before beginning any exercise program, check with your health care practitioner to make sure it is appropriate for you to undertake such a program. Follow all instructions carefully and be aware that using the weight training discussed in this book could involve risk, even though every effort has been made in the preparation of this book to stress the need for safety consciousness and proper techniques.

Acknowledgments

First, for their objective criticism of early drafts of our manuscript, we would like to thank William Blood and Dan Habib, head coaches in baseball and softball at Methuen High School, Methuen, Massachusetts. Thanks also to Ted Levesque for his sound advice and valuable input reflected in our chapter on softball pitching. We are indebted to Drs. Lorraine and Gerard Cassista for their help with our chapter on physical conditioning for softball. We are grateful to Michael Murray of Sports 28, Salem, New Hampshire, and Mark Farnham of Sparky Sports of Methuen, Massachusetts, for their answers to our questions on softball equipment.

For their fine work as demonstrators of sports technique, we wish to thank Tracie Petrie, Wendy Forgione, Jeff Coppeta, Jeremy Dziadosz, James Pagnoni, and Joseph Pagnoni. The excellent photographs were the work of John Mottern of Sherburne, Massachusetts.

Thanks also to the good people at Mountain Lion, Inc., especially John Monteleone, who helped shape the book into its present form.

Finally, thanks to our wives, Lesley Robinson and Carmela Pagnoni, who rearranged their schedules and patiently endured our writing sessions.

Foreword

With upwards of forty million players, softball can lay claim to being America's most popular team sport. Another twenty million men, women, boys and girls from around the world play softball. It is truly a game for the masses.

In the United States, nearly seven million boys and girls play softball in school and amateur athletic leagues. Much of the how-to information and fast-pitch play sections on these pages will be especially helpful to these young players and their coaches. Men who learned their basic playing skills from baseball and are now part of a slow-pitch league will be particularly interested in the sections on slow-pitch batting and pitching, running an efficient softball practice, and team fund raising.

Everyone will find useful the special sections on equipping a softball team, scoring a game, coaching a youth league team, and disputing an umpire's call (without getting thrown out in the process).

Play ball!

I. Physical Conditioning for Softball

As the largest team participation sport in America, softball is played just about everywhere: indoors and outdoors, all year round, by some 40 million people. But are those who play, children and adults, male and female, physically prepared to participate in the game without being injured? Many are not. As more and more people play softball, an increasing number of injuries occur; with proper conditioning before and during the season most of them could be prevented. Players tend to feel that they can simply switch off the television, grab their glove and cleats, run (or waddle, perhaps, after a winter of food storage!) to the local softball diamond, and be ready to play an injury-free ball game. Unfortunately, it doesn't work this way. Far too many injuries occur because out-of-shape players think that they can compete safely despite their physical condition.

Conditioning is important for all athletes, but, in general, the younger your players, the less they will need the programs that follow. A general fitness/conditioning program is beneficial for your softball team to help guard against nagging, painful, and sometimes debilitating injuries. The key to total fitness is a year-round conditioning program that promotes a healthy life-style—proper exercise, rest, and diet. Softball players who treat their bodies well all year long will find that their bodies treat *them* well during the season. Players who don't exercise throughout the year will enter the softball season at increased risk for injuries. They cannot expect to get in shape while playing softball; they must commit themselves to work year round at injury prevention. Those players who are still going strong at the season's end—diving for line shots, beating out ground balls, and running down drives in the outfield—are not just lucky or born that way. They are, more than likely, the well-conditioned, physically fit athletes who are able to shut the television off, put the potato chips away, and exercise regularly. Encourage your team to heed the advice of health experts: Regular conditioning pays off!

Flexibility/Stretching

The stretching exercises that follow are useful before and after a game and during the off-season. They are important, and so are the

1

warm-up drills that are done before stretching. It is necessary to work up a sweat by engaging in some aerobic exercise (such as jogging, biking, or walking briskly) to warm up the body before stretching. For a pregame workout, the stretching exercises should be done together as a team. It is not necessary to do every single one; pick and choose among them, and vary your selections. Make sure that your players stretch slowly and gently, and *never* bounce. Each person should know his limitations and stretch accordingly.

A caution: When stretching is done as a group, the tendency is to look at the person next to you and think, "If he or she can stretch that far, why can't I?" Make sure your players do not make the stretching routines a competition. This will only have harmful effects.

Shoulders/Arms

Standing with your feet apart, extend your arms to the side, and begin making small circles in a forward motion. Gradually increase the size of the circles. Finally, reverse the motion.

Triceps/Shoulders

1. Fold your arms above your head and grasp the elbow of one arm with the other hand. Pull the elbow behind your head, *slowly* and

FIGURE 1-1

CIRCLE STRETCHES: *Standing with feet apart, extend arms and make increasingly larger circles.*

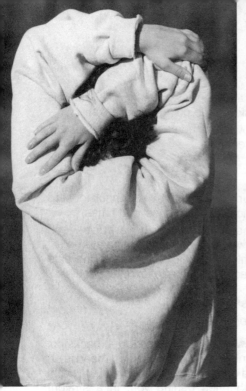 

FIGURE 1-2   **FIGURE 1-3**

TRICEPS/SHOULDER STRETCH: *The triceps and shoulders are stretched by pulling the elbow of one arm behind the head.*

FIGURE 1-4

SHOULDER STRETCH: *Stretch the shoulders by intertwining the fingers above the head and pushing back and up.*

gently. Reverse this process for the other elbow. A good addition is bending your hips from side to side while doing this exercise.

2. Intertwine your fingers above your head, with your palms up. Push back and up. Hold for 15 seconds.

Neck

1. Stand with your arms at your sides and push your neck forward with your chin down. Return to normal. Repeat several times.

2. Stand and look straight ahead. Move your head in slow and exaggerated "Yes" motions, followed by slow and exaggerated "No" motions. Next, still facing straight ahead, tilt your head to the side (left ear to left shoulder followed by right ear to right shoulder). Repeat several times.

Hips, Legs and Achilles Tendon

1. Stand a short distance away from a fence or a backstop, holding onto it with both hands, and lean forward until your head is on your arms. Bring one foot forward and put it down in front of you, with your knee bent. Extend the other leg behind you, in a straight position. Keeping your back flat, move your hips forward; remember to keep the back leg straight with the heel flat on the ground. Make this a *slow, easy* stretch with absolutely no bouncing. Repeat the same for the other leg.

2. Have two players face each other, an arm's length apart, then stretch their arms out forward, at eye level, and hold each other's hands. Have the players lean forward, bending their arms, until their foreheads touch. Hold this position briefly and then push back to an arm's length. Repeat this process three times.

Achilles Tendon/Ankle

1. Sit on the ground with your back straight and legs stretched out in front of you. Bend your ankles and stretch your toes back toward your knees. Repeat three times, holding for 10 seconds each time.

2. Sit on the ground, bend your left leg at the knee, and rotate your ankle clockwise 10 times, then 10 times counterclockwise. Do the same for the right ankle. Repeat three times for each ankle.

Hamstring

1. An excellent way to stretch the hamstring with a partner: One partner stands while the one who is stretching lies on his back with one leg raised and resting against his partner's thigh. The stretcher

FIGURE 1-5   **FIGURE 1-6**

ANKLE STRETCH: *Sitting on the ground with the back straight, bring one foot toward chest. Use your hand to provide resistance and rotate the ankle first in a clockwise and then in a counterclockwise motion.*

pushes hard against his partner's thigh (with the partner providing resistance) for a slow count of eight. After the eight count, the stretcher relaxes his leg muscles and his partner raises the leg about six inches higher. The stretcher starts pushing for another eight count, this time against the partner's stomach. The stretcher relaxes and the partner again raises the leg six inches to his chest. Continue stretching, relaxing, and raising the leg until the stretcher feels that he has reached his maximum stretch. Switch legs and start over. Finally, the partners swap places.

2. Sit on the ground with your right leg straight in front of you. Bend your left leg and place the sole of the foot against the inside of your right thigh. Be sure to keep the right leg straight and your foot and toes in an upright position. *Never* let the foot and toes of the straight leg drop to the side. Now, bend forward at the waist, sliding your hands down your straight leg toward your foot. To receive the full benefit of stretching the hamstring of the straight leg, concentrate on relaxing the quadriceps (the large muscle at the front of the thigh). Experts agree that it is easier to stretch the hamstring if the opposing muscle sets are relaxed. Repeat the exercise for the left leg.

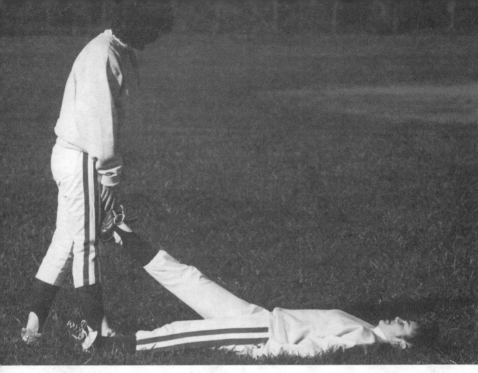

FIGURE 1-7

HAMSTRING STRETCH WITH PARTNER: *Place one leg on partner's thigh and push hard for a count of eight. Next, partner raises the leg six*

FIGURE 1-9

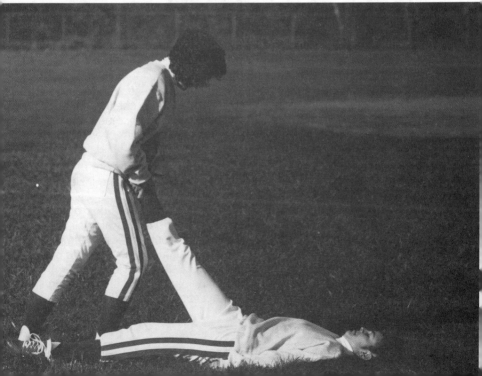

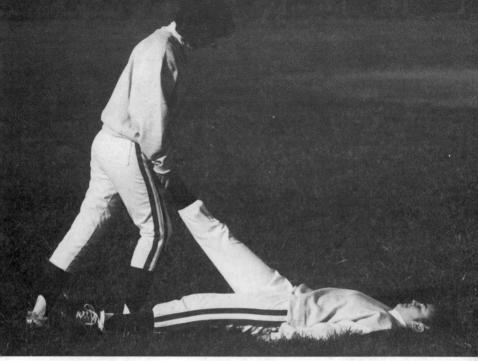

FIGURE 1-8

inches higher and repeats the process. The procedure continues until the maximum stretch has been reached..

Groin

1. Sit on the ground with the soles of your feet together. Hold onto your toes, pull yourself forward, and bend at the hip until you feel a stretch in the groin. Hold for 35 to 40 seconds. Don't bounce!

2. With a partner: Sit back to back, each with the soles of your feet together. Each of you pushes gently on your thighs (not your knees) and holds for 30 seconds.

Back

After stretching your groin (see above), lie on your back with your hands behind your head. Pull your knees up and put them together with your feet flat on the ground. Cross your left leg over your right and use it to push your right leg toward the ground until a stretch is felt in your hips and back. Hold for 30 seconds. Remember to keep your back flat and your hands behind your head. You do not have to touch your leg to the ground. Repeat for the other leg by crossing your right leg over your left.

FIGURE 1-10

HAMSTRING STRETCH: Bend forward at the waist, sliding hands down leg toward foot.

FIGURE 1-11

FIGURE 1-12

GROIN STRETCH: *With soles of feet together, hold onto toes and pull forward, bending at the hip until a stretch is felt in the groin area.*

Upper Body

Stand with your back to a chain-link fence or backstop. Extend your arms to the side and grab the fence at shoulder level. Lean forward and straighten your arms. Keep your chest out and your chin in. Hold for 10 seconds.

(Note: For additional information on flexibility for most sports, consult Bob Anderson's *Stretching*, Shelter Publications, Inc. This is generally considered the bible of stretching for athletics and everyday fitness.)

Endurance/Running

Running, bicycling, and rowing are all good builders of stamina and endurance and a good exercise program will include one or all three. Running is the most popular and easiest to implement but bicycling and rowing (including the stationary equipment) are also excellent conditioners. Almost all coaches include some running in their off-season programs: at least three days a week, several miles (or 15 to 20 minutes) per run. Some coaches prefer their players to include sprints (10 or 15 sprints at 30 or 50 yards each) in their running programs; others are satisfied with basic jogging over the required distance.

FIGURE 1-13

FIGURE 1-14

FIGURE 1-15

BACK STRETCH: *Lie on back with hands behind head. Pull feet up and cross one leg over the other, using it to push the other leg toward the ground until a stretch is felt in the hip and back.*

FIGURE 1-16

UPPER BODY STRETCH: With back to a chain link fence, grab the fence at shoulder level and lean forward.

FIGURE 1-17

Start your running program by walking briskly 2 to 4 miles for 3 to 4 weeks. The next stage should be a combination of walking and jogging over the same distance and time frame. Toward the end of this stage, you should be jogging more than walking. The final stage is jogging the entire route. At this point, you should find yourself running with comparative ease; an 8- to 10-minute mile is a good pace. When running, you should not push yourself; if you feel uncomfortable or winded, or if you have a nagging injury, stop for a few days. We advise runners to use the buddy system. Running with a partner keeps each of you bound to a regular routine and eases the tedium of that routine. A good indicator of conditioning is the ability to jog and carry on a normal conversation without becoming winded. Running should bring you peace and tranquility!

Research has shown that the best training effect takes place when the heart rate is between 70 and 80% of its maximum. As you would expect, our maximum heart rates decrease as we get older. By subtracting your age from 220, you can get a fairly accurate estimate of your maximum heart rate. Thus, a 15-year-old would use the equation $220 - 15 = 205$ to determine his maximum heart rate. Since 70 percent of 205 ($205 \times .7$) is 143.5, and 80 percent of 205 ($205 \times .8$) is 164, a 15-year-old might want to train at a heart rate between 144 and 164 heart beats per minute. He can monitor his heart rate by taking his pulse at the carotid arteries of the neck or at the wrist just above the thumb. The heart rate immediately after working out is basically the same as it was during the workout. So, an athlete can count his pulse beats for 15 seconds after working out for several minutes, multiply that figure by 4 to get his heart rate *per minute*, and gauge whether he is meeting his training requirement. He can then step up or slow down his workout based on whether he is below or above his target rate. Initially, 70 percent of maximum is a good target, but after training for a while, most athletes opt for working out at closer to 80 percent of maximum. Again, the workout should last at least 15 to 20 minutes (30 to 45 minutes or longer, if possible) and take place at least three times a week (daily, if possible).

Strength/Weight Training

The subject of weight training is a touchy one, especially when it concerns pre-adolescents and adolescents (generally, up to age 15). Weight training is not recommended for children under the age of 15 because irreparable damage may occur to the tendons and ligaments. Some coaches, when deciding when their players can begin weight training, adhere to the axiom: If you can shave, you can lift.

This works well for boys. Girls generally don't lift until they reach the high school varsity level. Those who do weight training undertake the same routines as boys, but work with lighter weights. You are likely to find that girls take to stretching readily but need to be coaxed to hit the weight training room. Boys, on the other hand, will usually stretch begrudgingly and lift happily ever after.

Once the decision has been made to lift, it is important to note that a set of muscles should be exercised three times a week. An athlete who is training every day should work on different parts of the body on different days of the week. A good off-season schedule, including weight training, aerobic exercise such as running, and stretching, would be to run on Monday, Wednesday, and Friday, lift on Tuesday, Thursday, and Saturday and take Sunday off. You should stretch every day. Heavy lifting should not be done during the season but is recommended for the off season. For example, pitchers should exercise their arms and shoulders daily with a weight training program during the off season but not during the season.

Initially, the weight trainer should limit himself to light weights, 10 to 15 minutes at a time, every other day, for 2 to 3 weeks. The eventual goal should be more repetitions, more sets, and increased length of workout (up to 30 to 60 minutes for the serious lifter). Concentrate on the large muscle groups of the leg, chest, back, stomach, neck, and shoulder. A sound weight training program involves repetitions (12 to 15) of three sets with a short rest between sets. When the third set becomes relatively easy to do, more weight can be added: an extra 5 pounds for your arms and 10 pounds for your legs and torso.

Weight Training Exercises

Athletes in all sports like the military press. Standing with the feet separated for good balance and the barbell in front of the chest, slowly extend the arms overhead. Hold briefly and return to the chest area. Remember—use light weights initially, and follow the progression suggested above.

A good upper body exercise is the bench press. For this routine, the lifter will need a bench (to lie on), uprights (to place the barbell on), and a barbell with weights. Place the weighted barbell in the uprights, lie on the bench, grasp the barbell, with palms up, and remove it from the uprights. Keeping the wrists straight, keep the bar an arm's length above you. Then, lower the bar until it barely touches your chest and return the bar to an arm's length distance. Repeat. It is important to use an assistant (spotter) in order to avoid the possibility of becoming trapped under the barbell and injured.

Flies or dumb flies are excellent exercises to develop the chest. The equipment needed here consists of two dumbbells and a bench.

FIGURE 1-18

MILITARY PRESS: *With the feet separated for balance, press the barbell slowly overhead and back down in front of chest.*

FIGURE 1-19

FIGURE 1-20
DUMB FLIES: Lie on a bench holding dumbbells, one in each hand, out to the side and slowly raise them overhead until they touch. Then return the dumbbells to the original position and repeat.
FIGURE 1-21

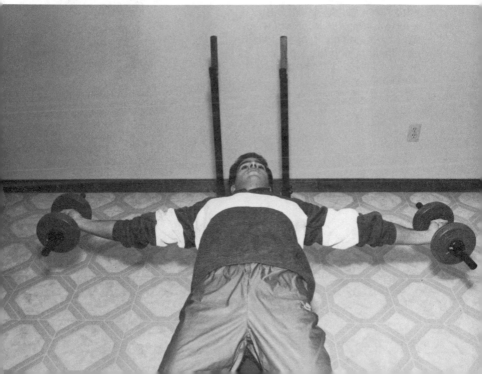

The lifter lies on the bench on his back and holds a dumbbell in each hand. He then extends his arms horizontally and slowly raises them above his chest until the dumbbells meet. Then he lowers his arms to the original position and repeats the exercise.

Wrist rollers are effective for developing the wrists and forearms. Drill a hole in a wooden bar (a heavy broomstick or rake handle cut to a 12- to 16-inch length works well) and slip a strong piece of rope (3 to 4 feet long) through it. Knot the end of the rope near the wooden bar and tie a weight (2½ to 5 pounds, depending on your size and strength) securely to the other end. Holding the bar out in front of you with the arms fully extended, use wrist action to wind the rope around the bar until the weight comes up to touch the handle. Then unwind the rope by twisting the handle in the opposite direction.

To strengthen the back, an exercise called the dumb row works well. Standing in front of a bench with feet 24 inches apart and knees slightly bent, the lifter leans forward and places his right hand on the bench. Keeping his chest parallel to the floor, he grabs the dumbbell in his left hand and raises it to his chest. He returns to original position and repeats. Then he repeats the exercise with the other arm.

Squats and toe presses are essential exercises for the legs and calf muscles. For the squats, equipment needed is the barbell, with

FIGURE 1-22

WRIST ROLLERS: *Extend the wooden bar out in front and wind the weight up until it meets the bar. Then unwind the rope, twisting the bar in the opposite direction.*

FIGURE 1-23

FIGURE 1-24

FIGURE 1-25

DUMBBELL ROW: Stand in front of a bench, place one hand on the bench and lift a dumbbell with the other. Raise the dumbbell to the chest and back down again, but do not let the weights touch the floor.

17

light weights optional. Place the barbell behind the head, while standing with heels on the floor. The lifter looks straight ahead, bends his knees, and lowers himself while keeping his back straight and the bar behind his head. He should go down only until his thighs are nearly parallel to the floor. (An alternative method is to go down until reaching the seat of a chair.) He returns to the original position and repeats. For the toe presses, the barbell is in the same position as for the squats. The lifter rises up on his toes and goes back down, being careful not to bounce or go too quickly, then repeats.

Using two dumbbells to do curls is a good way to develop the arms. With a dumbbell in each hand, raise one arm and curl the dumbbell, as if flexing the arm muscle. Return to the original position and repeat. Do the same routine for the other arm. Curls can also be done using the barbell with weights added. The barbell is curled up toward the chest while standing upright.

For those who reject formal weight training, there are other exercises that will build strength. A program that includes push-ups, pull-ups, and sit-ups will increase your strength. To develop strength

CURLS: *Using a barbell, curl the bar up toward chest while standing upright.*

FIGURE 1-26   **FIGURE 1-27**

in your hips, legs, and lower back (necessary for power hitting), you may do squats *without* putting weights on the barbell.

Additional exercises include movements that duplicate the actual movements of the game itself. For instance, a very good exercise to strengthen the arm (listen carefully, pitchers!) is to use a light weight dumbbell, imitating the underhand pitching motion. Swinging a weighted bat is another excellent exercise that will help develop a powerful swing. An interesting variation for this exercise is to use the weighted bat while hitting a ball off a batting tee. You should exercise caution when using these weighted implements since overuse or too heavy items may cause an injury. If you have had or are prone to shoulder, arm, or back injury, you should get a medical clearance from your physician.

Pregame/Prepractice Warm-up Program

A pregame warm-up program is necessary because it not only limbers up the team but also prepares them mentally for the game. Rather than having several activities going on at the same time or, worse, having some players not participate at all, the softball team should assemble for 10-20 minutes for the pregame warm-up. We recommend that the coach or team captains take the team through the following program, before practices as well as games:

1. Slow jog around perimeter of the field

2. Group stretching (emphasizing the groin, hamstring, neck, and back: see Flexibility/Stretching)

3. Calisthenics (e.g., push-ups, sit-ups, etc.)

4. Warm-up sprints—run 20-yard sprints in the outfield increasing speed with repetition

5. Game of catch (see Chapter III)

6. Infield/Outfield drill; optional for prepractice (see Chapters V and IX).

7. Pepper games and batting practice (see Chapter II and IX), if time allows.

8. Team meeting at end of session

This kind of group activity not only prepares the body for the game but also the mind. It is important that the players exercise and practice *together* as a team before a game; a feeling of camaraderie builds winning-caliber teams!

After each practice session and game, the team should have a cooling down period. A good cooling down technique is to have players choose one of the earlier stretching exercises and repeat it for about 5 minutes.

II. Hitting

Many people (including Ted Williams, who should know) have said that hitting a baseball is one of the most difficult skills in all of sport. While hitting slow-pitch softball is easier, hitting in fast-pitch softball is just as tough as—and sometimes tougher than—hitting in baseball. Hitting is a skill that requires concentration, timing, and confidence. Youngsters need to take a great deal of batting practice to develop that concentration and timing. And to help build that all-important confidence, a smart batting coach will add generous amounts of praise to the instructions he gives his hitters.

Bat Selection

To hit the ball with authority a player must use a bat that is the right weight for him. It is bat speed that drives the ball, so a hitter, particularly a young one, should select a bat that he can wield comfortably. The player may want to "choke up" on the bat to find the balance point at which the grip makes the swing smoothest and most comfortable. During the season, he may have to change to a heavier or lighter bat if his swings are consistently early or late.

A good test to determine if a young player is strong enough to swing a particular bat is to have him take the bat by the handle, with just one hand, and hold it out in front of him at arm's length, parallel to the ground, for 10 seconds. If he can manage this without wavering and straining, he will probably be able to swing that bat with authority and control.

The Mechanics of Hitting—Grip, Stance, Swing

Note: The following are general rules for hitting. But hitting is such an individual skill that some leeway must be given to hitters who are successful despite the fact that their technique is not textbook-perfect. The authors subscribe to the philosophy, "If it ain't broke, don't fix it!"

The hitter should pick up the bat as if it were an axe, with a right-handed hitter placing his left hand near the knob of the bat and his right hand above his left (reverse for a left-handed hitter). Hold the

FIGURE 2-1

BAT TEST: *If a youngster can hold a bat out at arm's length for ten seconds without wavering or straining, it is probably one she can swing with authority and control.*

bat near the middle of the fingers, not too far back in the palm of the hands. Grip the bat firmly but not too tightly, exerting pressure with the fingers, not the palms. Using batter's rosin makes for a more secure grip in sweaty hands. Today many players wear a batting glove on the lower hand, and some use them on both hands. Besides aiding grip, batting gloves help to prevent blisters and calluses; they also absorb some of the shock of bat-ball impact, which can really sting the hands, especially in cold weather.

In fast-pitch softball the hitter should stand just close enough to the plate so that he can reach the outside corner with his bat. He should hold the bat near the top of his strike zone (armpits) with his arms away from his body (but not fully extended). His belt buckle should be more or less in line with the center of home plate. He can move back in the box if the pitcher is fast, but getting back in the box tends to make breaking balls harder to hit. Moving up in the box can help your timing if the pitcher is slow, and also makes it possible to hit breaking stuff before it breaks. Some hitters like a closed stance (front foot closer to the plate than back foot), others like an open (opposite) one. A closed stance may help a hitter who tends to pull the ball foul and an open stance may help a hitter who swings later or

 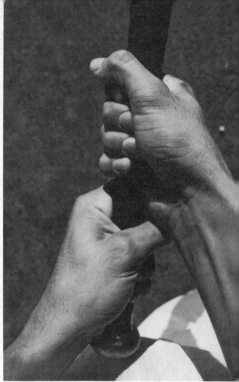

FIGURE 2-2   **FIGURE 2-3**

BAT GRIP: The bat is held near the middle of the fingers, not too far
back in the palm of the hands.

has trouble with inside pitches. It is important that the hitter's stride
be straight toward the pitcher and not toward third or first base. This
can help the hitter's timing as he tries to hit the ball straight back
through the box and to centerfield. For example, if a right-handed
hitter swings early he may hit to left field—if late, he may hit to right.

We teach our hitters to assume an athletic position. This is
balanced and kind of low (although most slow-pitch hitters tend to
have a fairly straight-up stance). The athletic stance is common to
many sports. A basketball player set to play defense, a linebacker
awaiting the snap of the football, or a tennis player set to return a
serve all have their weight forward on the balls of the feet, the feet
approximately shoulder width apart, and the body alert and ready to
move in any direction. We also prefer a somewhat wide stance that
will help the hitter take a relatively short stride (a 6-inch stride helps a
youngster keep his body in control during the swing). As the hitter
strides, he should throw the barrel of the bat out toward the ball.

A good drill to teach this is to let the hitters actually toss the bat at
an imaginary ball. You can do this as a mass hitting drill by lining your
players up along one foul line, each with his own bat. Keep the
players well separated and let each one feel the sensation of throwing
the bat's barrel at the ball.

FIGURE 2-4
ATHLETIC STANCE: *This athlete assumes an athletic stance with the weight forward on the balls of the feet, the feet approximately shoulder width apart, and the body alert and ready to move in any direction.*

FIGURE 2-5
BATTING STANCE: *Next, he takes a bat and puts it in the ready position.*

The hitter must see the ball as early as possible. He should try to "pick it up" as it leaves the pitcher's hand (fast-pitch softball hitters often key on the pitcher's hip or thigh or other "release zone," which is where the ball will come from) and try to track it until it hits his bat. Seeing the ball actually hit the bat has been deemed physically impossible in fast-pitch softball and baseball, but it is still good advice for young hitters. By attempting to see the ball hit the bat they are developing the visual tracking system that makes for a good hitter.

A good drill for picking up the ball quickly as the pitcher delivers it involves using colored (painted) balls. Use a pitcher, a catcher, and two hitters. The two hitters (one lefty and one righty would be ideal) take their normal batting stances without bats and compete to be first to correctly call out the color of the pitched ball.

As he swings, a good hitter needs to minimize his head movement to help steady his vision. Have your hitters put their chins on their front shoulders and swing. The body should rotate under the chin so that the chin ends up on the back shoulder. We advocate a number of important "dry" batting drills, done, like this one, without a ball. Do not underestimate the importance of such practice. With work, the skills developed can be transferred to live batting practice and game situations.

The ball must be batted out in front of the plate. In fact, the farther inside the pitch, the farther out in front of the plate the contact point must be. The farther the bat moves the more bat speed is generated, so the player wants to hit the ball out in front of the plate to get maximum bat speed. As he swings, he pivots on his back foot. This opens the hips and helps him "turn on the ball." Next comes a natural weight shift from back to front to help drive the ball. It is important to get a good weight transfer without lunging or overswinging at the ball. And it is critical not to try to pull outside pitches, but to hit them to the opposite field. The right-handed batter should hit outside pitches to right field and the left-hander should hit them to left field. Some youngsters tend to try to stop their swing just as contact with the ball is made. Encourage a smooth follow-through, keeping both hands on

MINIMUM HEAD MOVEMENT: *The hitter starts his swing with his chin on his front shoulder. As he completes his swing with a minimum of head movement, the chin ends up on his back shoulder.*

FIGURE 2-6   **FIGURE 2-7**

the bat. The hands should wrap around the lead shoulder with the bat ending up touching the middle of the hitter's back.

If possible, let your hitters watch their own swings in a mirror. A mirror may help a hitter see flaws in his technique that your verbal description may fail to conceptualize for him. The videotape camera is another terrific tool for training hitters, as well as for most aspects of any sport. If you have access to one, use the slow motion and stop-action features to help your hitters see and understand the problems with their swings.

If you do not have access to video, don't despair. There are many simple but effective drills that you can use without high technology. One is for kids to hit fungoes to each other. (Fungo hitting involves tossing the ball into the air with one hand and then hitting it to a teammate.) You will probably be surprised at how ineffective young-sters are at hitting grounders and flies to each other but the activity makes them work on their hand-eye coordination as well as on seeing the ball hit the bat.

Since the swing is so vital in hitting ("the swing's the thing!" as many coaches say), hitters may benefit during indoor and outdoor practices by batting whiffle balls, sock balls, or even paper balls. Have your players tie up old socks in knots and hack away at them. Do the same thing with rolled-up and taped newspaper. Your players can hit them off tees outdoors, in the gym, or even in the garage or cellar in the off-season. They might hit into an old sheet suspended from the ceiling.

Or players can hang an old tire up by a rope and pound on it (as little as 10 minutes a day will strengthen wrists and forearms considerably). But teach them not to flail away at the tire mindlessly. They should imagine pitches in various locations (low, inside corner, then waist-high, outside corner, etc.) and take their best swings. Another popular practice mode involves tying a sock or paper ball to a string suspended from the garage or cellar ceiling. Now they are hitting a moving ball.

In all your hitting drills, emphasize trying to hit line drives and hard ground balls, not fly balls.

The Mental Aspects of Hitting

To be successful, a hitter must be confident and mentally aggres-sive at the plate, even if he is mired in a prolonged slump. In fast-pitch softball he should be "thinking swing" as the pitch is delivered and be prepared to abort the swing if the pitch is not to his liking. For example, his mental approach on every pitch should be something like this: "I'm going to hit it—I'm going to hit it... No! That was a ball."

A good hitter doesn't get cheated by taking strikes because he is indecisive at the dish. He takes his cuts.

Always use batting helmets even during bunting practice and even if your pitchers are not throwing hard. A youngster who gets hit with a pitch often loses confidence at the plate. (Consider using tennis balls or whiffle balls for batting practice with beginning players.) When the junior author was playing American Legion baseball as an 18-year-old, he had an experience that drove home the importance of confidence in batting. One of his teammates was a hot-shot soccer star but only a mediocre baseball player and a downright weak hitter. But he was so cocky and sure of himself (a by-product of his soccer prowess) that he went up to the plate, exuding confidence. He knew that he was good and he knew that the pitcher couldn't get him out. His belief in himself sent him up to the dish swinging and roping line drives.

Similarly, sometimes a player will find what he believes is a flaw in his swing. Though the flaw is imaginary and the correction of it only mental, his belief that he has cured his batting woes sends him on a batting tear. Belief in yourself brings confidence at the plate—and there's no substitute for it.

A hitter's goal has to change depending on the game situation during each at-bat. He must be an "on-er," a "mover," or a "producer." If he is the lead-off hitter in an inning, he becomes an on-er. His job is to reach base any way he can (hit, error, walk, etc.). The chances of the team scoring increase dramatically if the lead man reaches base. If he bats with men on base and less then two outs, he may be called upon to be a mover. His job now is to push the runners around so that teammates can drive them in. For example, with a runner on second and no outs, the hitter's job is to get that runner to third, say, with a ground ball to the right side. A runner on third with one out can score in many ways in softball (especially fast-pitch softball). If there are runners in scoring position, the hitter's job is to drive them in. He becomes the producer, the RBI person. This is the time to open up the strike zone a little and become even more aggressive at the plate.

Note: We believe that the old adage, "A walk is as good as a hit," is wrong for youth sports; in fact it may be one of the greatest fallacies in children's athletics. If you want kids to learn to hit, you have to encourage them to swing the bat. Nothing is more boring for the players, spectators, and umpires than a game that consists of walk after walk. You can win the ball game this way, but the kids aren't really learning and nobody's having fun. We try to teach kids to swing at good pitches, not just at anything that comes up there, but at the same time to be aggressive and take their cuts. We want them in the mind set that *a hit is better than a walk.*

Generally, with no strikes a hitter should be fussy and wait for a good pitch to hit. This doesn't necessarily mean he should always lay off the first pitch. Most pitchers want to get ahead in the count and throw a fastball for a strike on the first pitch. This is often a good pitch to hit. The hitter must concentrate on laying off the high stuff and the breaking balls in the dirt. Good pitches to hit are when the hitter is ahead in the count and can expect a fast ball for a strike. These include our favorite hitting pitches, 2-0 and 3-1. This is when coaches tell their hitters to "look in the wheelhouse" for a pitch to drive. Some coaches tell hitters in this situation to look for their pitch in their favorite location. With two strikes we want our hitters to just try to make contact up the middle. Their goal always is to be a tough out.

We also tell our youngsters "Never swing at a pitch that fools you, just take the pitch, unless you have two strikes." We want them to remember to hit the outside pitch to the opposite field and to think about getting "on top of the ball" (hitting the top half of the ball) to hit grounders and liners instead of lazy fly balls. Bat control and bat speed are crucial. Your hitters must strive for a short, compact swing which makes it easier to control timing. By hitting often and working on these points your players will develop a good visual tracking system that allows them to pick up the ball early, follow it to the bat, and hit it hard. With repeated practice they will develop what coaches call "muscle memory," so that hitting properly becomes a reflex.

To a great extent, how hard your players work at hitting will determine how much success they have. Convince them that other players may be bigger, stronger, or quicker, but time and effort are great equalizers in skill development. Of course good coaching is a vital factor in this equation. That's where you come in.

Dry Batting Drills

Dry Swings

Done individually or as a mass drill (entire team at once), this drill requires players to swing at imaginary pitches in different locations. The coach calls out "Low and outside strike" or "High, inside strike," and each player looks in that location in his personal strike zone and takes a good cut at an imaginary ball.

One-Hand Swings

For this drill each player swings the bat at an imaginary ball but with only one hand, first using the bottom hand and then using the top hand. Using only the bottom hand makes the batter work on his

FIGURE 2-8

FIGURE 2-9

FIGURE 2-10

BOTTOM HAND SWINGS:
Swinging with just the bottom hand makes the batter work on his front arm extension and driving force.

FIGURE 2-11

FIGURE 2-12

FIGURE 2-13

TOP HAND SWINGS: *Swinging with just the top hand develops bat control in the swing.*

front arm extension and driving force, while using only the top hand develops bat control in the swing.

Rapid Swings

Using both hands, players swing hard and repeatedly at an imaginary ball and in rapid succession. They are working on bat speed as well as conditioning the forearms and wrists. Even the biceps and triceps get a good workout in a short time with this exercise.

Live Batting Drills

Pepper

Pepper is a fine drill that develops hand-eye coordination as well as bat control, and includes fielding work, too. One batter hits to several fielders who stand about 20 feet away. The batter doesn't take a full swing, concentrating more on solid contact and place-hitting. The player who fields the batted ball tosses it back to the batter, who hits it again. You might make the hitter focus on hitting ground balls by making any hit caught on the fly end his turn at bat. The player who made the catch comes to bat.

Another variation is to have the player at the farthest end of the fielding line be "on deck." As soon as three successive balls are fielded without an error the on-deck hitter is up, and the other fielders move up a position toward the on-deck spot. The batter goes to the end of the fielding line. Any error starts the three-out count over and sends the player who made the miscue to the end of the line.

Batting Tees

Next to videotape equipment, a batting tee is the best teaching tool for young hitters. Tees can be purchased or made very easily by cementing a 3-foot length of 1½-inch-diameter pipe into a can. Fasten a rubber hose or tubing to the pipe to hit off and you're in business. The tee is ideal for practicing swinging at a stationary target in different parts of the strike zone. You can raise and lower the rubber hose to adjust the height of the pitch and players can move closer to or farther away from the tee to simulate inside and outside pitches. They can hit at fielders or against a screen.

Players need time to take to this form of practice. They would rather face live pitching and they get frustrated when they hit the tubing (which is common at first). Encourage them to stay with it, though, and they will benefit greatly.

FIGURE 2-14

FIGURE 2-16

FIGURE 2-15

FUNGO HITTING: Hitting fungoes to teammates makes a hitter work on hand-eye coordination as well as seeing the ball hit the bat.

FIGURE 2-17 **FIGURE 2-18**

BATTING TEE: *The batting tee is ideal to practice swinging at a stationary target in different parts of the strike zone.*

Soft Toss

In this drill players work in pairs: one tosses the ball and the other bats it. It is best to use whiffle, sock, or paper balls (if you use real balls, have the tosser wear a catcher's mask). The tosser feeds balls underhand to his partner 5 feet away. The tosser is on one knee and at a 45-degree angle to the hitter. An alternate position for the tosser is directly across from the hitter and opposite his back foot. His tosses must be out in front of the hitter's lead foot to insure that the pitch is in the proper hitting zone, and also that the ball is not hit back at him. Another alternative is to get the hitter down on one knee too. This reduces uppercutting and makes him focus on swinging with wrists and forearms, the key components of a controlled swing. After the player has hit a bucket of balls the two players change positions.

If you use real balls, avoid hitting against the backstop to prevent injuries to the hitter and tosser from balls that hit support pipes and bounce back at them. (The repeated impact of balls can also damage the backstop.) The best way to do soft toss with real balls is to combine it with fielding. Have groups hitting from each foul line and station fielders in position to make the plays. Soft toss may also be done using one-hand swings, as described earlier. Still another

FIGURE 2-19

FIGURE 2-20

FIGURE 2-21

SOFT TOSS USING WHIFFLE BALLS: *The tosser kneels and feeds balls underhand to his partner. After hitting a bucket of balls, the players switch positions.*

FIGURE 2-22

SOFT TOSS—ONE KNEE: *Soft toss on one knee makes the hitter focus on swinging with the wrists and forearms, which are the key ingredients of a controlled swing.*

variation is soft toss with no stride. Have the hitters spread their feet as if they have already taken their stride. Now they can hit soft toss, again concentrating solely on upper-body mechanics.

(Note: See Chapter IX for instructions on running conventional as well as alternative batting-practice sessions.)

Common Hitting Errors

Head Turning

Youngsters who turn their heads away from the ball when they swing often "step in the bucket" and are sometimes afraid of being hit by the pitch. You can help them overcome this fear by making sure they wear batting helmets and give them practice in getting out of the way of a pitch by throwing tennis balls at them. They should practice turning their backs to the ball (turning toward the catcher) and falling straight down to the ground. This type of fall protects the head, face, and vital organs. A player should take his bat down with him to prevent the ball from hitting it.

Head turners should shorten their stride or get farther away from the plate. They can also work on hitting to the opposite field. Have them spend additional time hitting fungoes to drill them on seeing the ball hit the bat. Some head turners are just overswinging. Have them take a little off those big cuts.

Overstriding

Youngsters who overstride have their body weight already forward by the time they strike the ball. When the body weight shifts ahead of the swing, the batter lunges at the ball and loses power in his swing. He might adjust by starting out with a somewhat wider stance and concentrating on a short (6-inch) stride. Try to make sure that the hitter's weight shift is against a firmly planted front foot.

Uppercutting

Make a hitter who uppercuts keep his lead elbow down and swing through the ball. Players should hit the top half of the ball for ground balls and line drives, not fly balls, which are easy outs.

For many young hitters, inability to hit is not a mechanical problem. Their technique is fine; it is their timing that is off. They swing late because they are not alert and aggressive, or because the pitcher is overpowering them. Make sure they are alert and ready with a short, compact swing. Just as often good hitters make no contact because they swing too early. By the time the ball enters the sweet zone they are already into their follow-through. Encourage youngsters to "wait on the ball" and to "see it a little longer" before swinging. Hitting is the toughest thing to do in sports. Just keep working at it.

Bunting (Fast-pitch Softball Only)

The little bunt is a big weapon. This is a fundamental truth of softball, and the sooner your players understand it the better off your team will be. Bunting is an essential skill. Some coaches go so far as to say that the weaker a player's hitting, the stronger his bunting must be. At one time or another every player, even your team's power hitter, will probably be called upon to sacrifice himself to get an important run into scoring position. Make sure everyone understands this at the outset. Do what's best for the team, regardless of personal statistics. Simply stated, we say, "Big team, little me!"

The Sacrifice Bunt

The notion of the sacrifice bunt is that you are giving yourself up to gain an advantage for the team. When you get a runner into scoring position with a successful bunt, your chance of scoring one run increases significantly, but your chance for a big inning decreases. Your players must fully understand this to accept the importance of their jobs. Given the fielding ability of most low- and intermediate-level teams, a bunt is likely to be successful without even giving up an out. The defense is likely to butcher the play, leaving all runners safe. Until a team shows us that it can defend the sacrifice bunt successfully, we often continue to bunt. For example, if we bunt with a runner on first with no outs and the defense gets neither runner (giving us runners at first and second with no outs), we are inclined to bunt again, especially if we are near the bottom of the batting order.

The player must bunt strikes. It is especially important to lay off high pitches which tend to be popped up and, with bad baserunning, can lead to a double play. Train baserunners in a sacrifice bunt situation not to run until the bunted ball is on the ground. Keep the ball away from the pitcher, bunting toward third or first. In either case, the primary target is a few feet inside the foul lines and about 15 feet from home plate. We want our bunters to "square around early and run late." It is more important for a bunter to get into good bunting position than it is to surprise the defense. It doesn't do any good to jump around at the last second, fooling everybody but fouling off the pitch in the process. Many bunters fail to get a good bunt down because they start running to first before they have actually bunted the ball. Remember, the hitter is sacrificing himself. His job is to get the runner into scoring position. If, after getting a good bunt down, he then runs to first and beats the throw, it is a bonus.

Always praise the successful bunter. Make as big a deal of his sacrifice bunt as you do of the hit that drives in the run. This will send a clear message to everybody about how important bunting is to you.

Mechanics of Bunting

The bunter must square around to face the pitcher. We recommend two ways of accomplishing this. One is to face the pitcher by taking a quick step forward with the front foot, followed by a step with the back foot which brings the bunter square with the pitcher. Make sure that neither foot (usually the back one) touches the plate or the batter will be out if he *hits* the ball, fair or foul. Squaring around in this manner brings the hitter well in front of home plate, which increases his chance of bunting the ball into fair territory. As he squares around, he must slide his hands down the bat so that the top hand ends up near the label. He should pinch the bat firmly with the fingers of the top hand rather than wrap them around the bat and risk getting hit by the pitch. He must hold the bat well out toward the pitcher and over the plate (which is somewhat farther away from him now that he is in bunting position). The bunter must hold the bat parallel to the ground and at the top of the strike zone (the armpits). If the ball is higher than the bat, it is out of the strike zone and should not be bunted. The hands should be about a foot apart, with the lower hand a bit more relaxed than the upper. A good teaching aid for beginners is to put tape on the bat in the general area where you want the bunter's hands to grip the bat during bunting.

The trick now is to let the ball hit the bat rather than to lunge at or bunt at the ball. Some coaches talk about "catching the ball with the bat" to get this across to their players. The bunter should stay in his athletic stance, bend his knees for low strikes, and lay off the high pitches. A slight movement forward or back with the bottom hand will direct the ball toward first or third base.

HAND POSITION DURING BUNT: *The bunter pinches the bat firmly with the fingers of the top hand rather than wrapping them around the bat and risking getting hit by the pitch.*
FIGURE 2-23

The second method we teach to get a player into position to bunt is to have him pivot on the balls of both feet simultaneously. He simply points his toes at the pitcher and shortens up on the bat as previously described. He must get the bat parallel to the ground, at the top of the strike zone and out over the plate, while extending his arms well toward the pitcher. This method is recommended because it is easy for youngsters to learn, prevents them from stepping on the plate, and gives them the option to fake bunt and slash. This can be added to your offensive strategy once the sacrifice bunt has been mastered. The idea is to pivot around and, when the pitch is delivered, quickly pivot back into hitting position and take a short swing or slash at the ball, trying to drive it past or over the head of a charging infielder.

PIVOT BUNT: *The bunter pivots on both feet simultaneously, keeping the bat at the top of the strike zone and out over the plate. The arms are extended toward the pitcher. This technique is ideal for the fake bunt and slash maneuver.*

FIGURE 2-24

DRAG BUNT: *The element of surprise is critical to the success of the drag bunt. The bunter waits until the last instant as the pitch is in flight. He drops the right foot back and bends the left knee while dropping the bat over the plate in a "chopping wood" motion.*

FIGURE 2-25

Drag Bunt

The drag bunt is not a sacrifice. You do not square around and you do not wait until the ball is on the ground before running to first. You are bunting for a base hit and the element of surprise is important. The right-handed hitter must wait until the last instant as the pitch is in flight, then drop the right foot back and bend the left knee while dropping the bat over the plate in a "chopping wood" motion. He pushes off on the right foot immediately and takes off for first. A well-placed bunt is right down the third base line.

A left-handed batter executing this bunt will cross his left leg over his right and extend his bat over the plate. Contact with the ball and taking off for first are more or less simultaneous. Try to keep this bunt away from the pitcher, preferably toward the first baseman.

Another type of bunt that is ideal for talented players with good speed and equally good bat control is the push bunt. The batter squares around late and bunts the ball hard toward second base. (Gripping the bat tightly will make the ball travel farther.) The trick is to get the ball past the pitcher so that the second baseman must play the ball. This makes for a very tough chance for the second sacker as he has to charge a slow roller and then throw across his body to retire a speedy baserunner.

Bunting Drills

Mass Bunting (Dry)

Each player must have a bat and glove. Spread the players out and have each place his glove on the ground to serve as home plate. On your command, the players square around into good bunting position and hold until you get around to observe flaws and make comments. Walk around, quickly looking for errors and pointing them out. "Sue, your bat should be up higher, at the top of your strike zone...That's fine, Nancy...Sarah, extend your arms well out toward the pitcher...Be careful when you square around, Tanya, your back foot is almost touching the plate. ..." Repeat this drill several times and you can get in a lot of teaching in a short time. With each repetition there should be fewer corrective comments and more praise for jobs well done. It is a good idea to use this just before a live bunting drill. You can alter this drill to work on the technique for drag and push bunts as well.

Bull's-Eye Bunting

Set up targets for the bunter to aim at. Use cones or bats to designate sweet spots for good bunts down the first and third base lines. This can be made into a competitive drill where points are scored for good bunts and, if you wish, deducted for foul or poorly bunted balls (e.g., right back to the pitcher). Use the drill for sacrifice bunts as well as for bunts for base hits.

Small Group Bunting

Set up groups of three or four players each. One player is the bunter, one the pitcher, and one or two fielders simulate first and third basemen. The pitchers and bunters should be about 20 feet apart. Each bunter bunts five, then all players rotate within their group. After all have sacrifice bunted, drag bunt and push bunt on the next two rounds. Use home plates for this drill if you have them, otherwise use the bunter's glove as the plate.

Single-Line Bunting

Set up one bunter and a single line of four or five players, each with his own softball. The first player in the line pitches to the bunter from about 20 feet away, then charges and fields the bunted ball. After retrieving the ball, he runs to the end of the line. On the coach's whistle or after every fielder has pitched and fielded his ball or after a set number of bunts, the bunter switches places with one of the fielders, who takes his place at the plate. The moment one fielder has retrieved his bunted ball and started on his way toward the end of the line, the next ball should be pitched. This drill allows for a lot of bunts in a short time and keeps everybody hustling.

Hitting in Slow-pitch Softball

We said earlier that hitting slow-pitch softball is easier than hitting fast-pitch softball. Let us clarify: Slow-pitch softball is easy to hit. But it isn't so easy to hit well, especially when the pitcher knows his craft. It is critical that slow-pitch players understand the strike zone before they can even think of becoming good hitters. A legally pitched ball must reach a height of 6 to 12 feet from the ground. If the arc is higher than 12 feet or lower than 6 feet, the umpire is supposed to call "Illegal pitch!" at the time the pitch becomes illegal. The illegal pitch will be an automatic ball on the batter unless he swings at it, in which case the pitch becomes legal. To be a called strike, any part of the legally pitched ball must pass through any part of the strike zone (defined in the Amateur Softball Association's Official Playing Rules as "that space over any part of home plate between the batter's back shoulder and his knees when he assumes a natural batting stance.") Whether the batter moves up or back in the box has no bearing on his strike zone. Umpires call the strike zone as if the batter were directly at the plate.

As a practical matter, umpires generally judge balls and strikes by where the ball lands. Some draw an imaginary line anywhere from 12 to 24 inches (or more) behind the plate. Balls hitting within that area and within the width of the plate are strikes. Pitches falling beyond the imaginary line are ruled "deep" and are balls. Pitches must pass the point of the plate where the triangular section begins and pitches that hit the plate can never be called strikes. Most umpires will call a pretty liberal strike zone to try to keep the game moving. In fact, we once heard a high-ranking A.S.A. official declare at a rules clinic that the slow-pitch softball strike zone is "Strike one, strike two, ya better be swinging!" A pitch that lands several inches inside or outside the plate may be ruled a strike because its trajectory may have carried it through the strike zone. In other words, even though it fell to the ground, say, 14 inches behind the plate and 3 inches outside, it was on the corner and in the strike zone when it passed over the plate.

So how should the batter approach hitting in the slow-pitch game? First off, the fundamentals of hitting we outlined earlier hold true for slow-pitch softball, except that most slow-pitch hitters favor a fairly straight-up stance. The tendency in slow-pitch softball is to undercut the ball (like a golf swing) because the hitter is trying to lift the ball over the outfielders' heads. As in fast-pitch softball, the best swing is straight through the ball, targeting on the top half of the ball so as to hit grounders and liners. The swing is level or even slightly downward. Hitters should take a full swing but leave the home-run cut for those big guys with rippling biceps and powerful wrists.

If your batters are good at hitting low pitches, get them back in the box. If they are high-ball hitters, move them up. As umpires, we are amazed at the different pitches hitters "jump on" and hit for extra bases. A pitch that we would take for a ball someone hits out of the park. Pitches that we would love to swing at get taken for strikes. The point is that your hitters have to know which pitches *they* can hit solidly, and must try to have the patience to wait for one. Of course, they must determine their best hitting pitches during batting practice.

Too many hitters are reluctant to hit with strikes on them, so they flail away at the first pitch they see. Think of it this way. The pitch with a 12-foot arc is going to take maybe one and a half seconds to reach the plate. The hitter has time to size it up and decide if it is a ball that he can hit well. Slow-pitch softball produces very few strike-outs. Since the hitter is probably not going to strike out, he can be patient, selective. He will get at least three pitches to choose from. He must pick the one he can drive, then hit it where it is pitched—pull the inside pitch, hit the outside pitch to the opposite field. With two strikes he must "protect the plate," which means swing at anything that the umpire could possibly call a strike. If your league uses the A.S.A. two-strike rule (any foul ball hit with two strikes on the batter is an out), the batter must concentrate on hitting the ball up the middle of the infield. Teach your players to watch the game carefully, to be keen observers—and to use whatever information they can garner. What can they learn about the umpire's strike zone? Does he call deep strikes? Is he reluctant to bang players out on strike three? Does the pitcher throw a low arc when he is behind in the count?

As in fast-pitch softball and baseball, fly balls and pop-ups are such routine outs that they are to be avoided if at all possible. On the other hand, a ground ball requires one player to field it and throw it accurately and another player to catch it and either step on a bag or tag a runner—all in a restricted time frame (before the runner beats the play). In addition, a play at the bases gives the umpire his chance to butcher the play. So, concentrate on hitting line drives and hard ground balls.

Most successful slow-pitch hitters stand deep in the batter's box and away from the plate. Standing deep in the box lets you hit a ball that is below shoulder level, which you can hit on the line or on the ground. Getting away from the plate lets you hit the inside pitch hard and the outside pitch to the opposite field. If the pitcher throws with a low arc (say, 6 to 8 or 9 feet), then it may be advantageous to move up in the box since these pitches drop off quickly as they reach the plate. You may find yourself swinging at very low pitches (which are strikes) if you remain deep in the box.

A word of caution about moving around in the batter's box. You are out if you step on the plate and hit the ball (fair or foul). You are also out if you step completely out of the batter's box with your foot on the ground when you hit the ball (fair or foul). For this latter play to be an out, all three conditions must be met: foot completely out of the box, on the ground, while the ball is hit. Most batters called out for being out of the batter's box in slow-pitch softball are trying to hit the ball to the opposite field. They lunge toward the opposite field with their front foot. In fast-pitch softball, we sometimes see a left-handed batter who is bunting for a base hit start running to first before he has made contact with the ball. By the time the bat hits the ball, he is well out of the box—and ruled out by an alert umpire.

In slow-pitch softball it is extremely important to be able to hit to the right side of the diamond. Since there is no bunting or stealing, hitting "behind the runner" is one of the few ways to advance teammates around the bases. Bat control may be even more important than in fast-pitch softball because good slow-pitch players must be able to hit the ball to a specific area. Place hitting allows them to direct the ball to open areas or to weak fielders. Some hitters will drop the rear foot back as the pitch is delivered to position themselves to hit to the opposite field. Of course, there is another school of thought that says to forget about place hitting. It is difficult to do consistently well, and young hitters would be better of just concentrating on hitting the ball down and hard, rather than cluttering their minds with concerns about where the ball will go after it is hit. (For more on the strategies of slow-pitch batting see Chapter XI.)

III. Throwing

One of the first things we teach our players is how to play catch. Sure, everyone can play catch. But we have a specific method that warms up the arms and insures correct throwing and fielding mechanics. Throwing properly promotes accuracy and velocity; it also reduces the chance of injury.

First, we want our players warming up in the outfield, either in left field, throwing parallel to the second and third base line, or in right field, throwing parallel to the first and second base line. This gives the players plenty of room to spread out, gets everyone throwing along the same plane so that balls are not flying in all directions, and prevents digging up the infield.

Next, the grip. Players should grip the ball across the seams with two, three, or four fingers depending on their age and the size of their hands. They should hold it firmly, but not too far back in the palm of their hands. There should be a space between the ball and the palm that allows light to pass through easily.

Throws should be overhanded (most youngsters throw about three quarters overhand and this is acceptable). Sometimes sidearm throws are called for in the infield, but never in the outfield. An infielder charging a slow roller may want to stay low and throw quickly from a sidearm position, and sometimes pivot men on double-play balls must throw sidearm. But sidearm tosses are generally among the least accurate throws that young players make and should be avoided whenever possible.

The thrower should sight on the target. Of course, in playing catch the intended receiver is the target. But we always have our receivers give a target (see photo). The receiver holds his glove and throwing hand up as if he were surrendering in a holdup. The thrower aims for the receiver's chest, although anywhere between the head and the knees is acceptable.

We have a hard-and-fast rule: **No one is to throw to a teammate who fails to give a proper target**. This averts injuries, because it can sometimes appear that a teammate is looking right at you and expecting a throw and the next thing you know he takes a ball off the head. When a teammate gives a throwing target, he is telling you that he is ready to receive a strong, accurate throw.

After catching the ball, the player should bring his glove and ball to his chest area toward the throwing shoulder. He should separate his

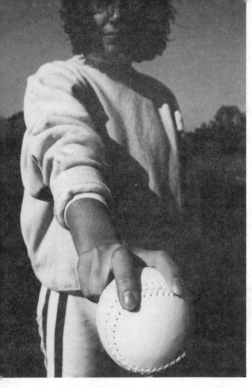

FIGURE 3-1

TWO FINGER GRIP: *The ball is gripped with two fingers across the seams. It is held firmly, but not too far back in the palm of the hand.*

THREE FINGER GRIP (TWO VIEWS): *Players with smaller hands like the three finger grip.*

FIGURE 3-2

FIGURE 3-3

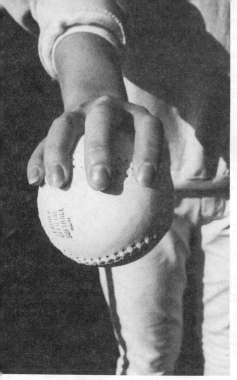 

FIGURE 3-4   **FIGURE 3-5**

FOUR FINGER GRIP (TWO VIEWS): *Players with the smallest hands may use the four finger grip.*

FIGURE 3-6

TARGET: *Throw only to a teammate who is giving a proper target. This will prevent injuries.*

FIGURE 3-7

THROWING MOTION: *The thrower brings the ball and glove to the chest area. He separates the hands, points the glove in the direction of the target, steps toward the target, and makes a strong accurate throw.*

hands, point his glove toward the target and begin his step in the direction of the target. At this point his body weight is mostly on the back foot. He should keep his throwing elbow high (shoulder height) and his arm extended well above his head. The throw is completed with a strong wrist snap as the ball is released. The glove hand should drive downward and the throwing hand comes all the way down past the glove-side (front) knee. During the follow-through, the body weight transfers to the front foot, and the back foot comes off the ground and forward slightly as the body "rolls" into the finish position.

Many players like to "crow hop" before they throw, as it gets them into a rhythm and adds momentum to their throws. A right-hander, after catching the ball, would hop on his right foot, then step toward the target with his left foot and release the ball. No time is wasted during the crow hop, as it is made while the ball and glove are being brought to the chest to begin the throw.

We start our players off throwing gently to a partner who is close (15 to 20 feet away). They back up gradually, throwing progressively harder as the arms loosen up, until they are throwing hard from a

FIGURE 3-8

FIGURE 3-9

distance of 60 to 100 feet or farther (depending on their age and ability). Players can gauge the distance by glancing over at the baseline. The bases are 60 feet apart in fast-pitch softball and 65 feet apart in slow-pitch softball.

Coaching Points to Emphasize

When fielding a thrown or batted ball, bring the ball and glove to the throwing side shoulder, separate the hands, point the glove and guide shoulder (glove-side) at the target, take a step toward the target, and release a strong, accurate throw.

Be sure that the players keep their fingers on top of the ball, during both the backswing and the release. The fingers should never be underneath, like a waiter carrying a serving tray.

Most beginners tend to throw the ball too high, especially from the outfield. We like our players to throw with as flat an arc as possible. Throw the ball low and hard, especially from the outfield, where throws on one bounce are not only acceptable, but encouraged.

A common error for young players is to toss the ball and abruptly stop their arm's forward motion at the release point, as if throwing a dart. Impress upon them the importance of a smooth release and a follow-through directed straight at the target.

We want our players to catch the ball with two hands. They're less likely to drop it and they'll get off a quicker throw. When you catch with two hands, your throwing hand is in good position to make the transition from catching to throwing. Catching with one hand requires an extra movement, that of reaching into the glove and securing the ball.

Another thing we emphasize in playing catch is "looking the ball into the glove." We want our players to follow the path of the ball right into the web of the glove, so we constantly remind them to "look it in," to make their eyes follow the ball *all the way* into the glove. They complete the catch by cushioning the ball (giving slightly with its impact) and bringing it to the belt area (on a ground ball), then finally to the chest area. Fielders who cushion the ball well on impact are said to have "soft hands" and make solid defensive players.

Finally, we try to teach our charges when *not to throw*. In game situations, most youth leaguers make unnecessary throws—throwing to a base, for example, when there is little chance of getting an out. It is difficult to teach youngsters when to throw and when to "swallow it" to prevent further damage. Lots of practice, game-time experience, and communication from teammates will develop the instincts needed for good judgment in knowing when and when not to throw.

"Striper" Drills for Throwing Mechanics

Youngsters' throws often sail and tail off in all directions because their throwing motion imparts strange spins to the ball. A way to see and correct these spins is to use striped or painted balls. Use a strip of black electrical tape to make a single stripe around a softball. A player using the three-finger grip (and holding the ball so that the stripe is vertical) would hold the ball with the middle finger on the tape, one finger on either side of the tape, and the thumb under the ball and on the tape. The idea is to "throw a striper," a ball that clearly shows one vertical black stripe as it flies through the air. With practice, youngsters can correct errors in their throwing mechanics that caused strange spins and wobbling stripes. The idea is to examine the rotation of the ball by watching the stripe. Coloring or painting half of the ball will make for the same teaching aid (during flight, the two colors should remain on opposite sides of the ball).

STRIPER GRIP: *Using the three finger grip, the player holds the ball with the middle finger on the tape, one finger on either side of the tape, and the thumb under the ball and on the tape.*

FIGURE 3-10

FIGURE 3-11
ONE KNEE STRIPER: *Partners, 15 to 25 feet apart, work on throwing stripers while on one knee.*

Statue of Liberty Drill

Each player has a throwing partner. He places the elbow of his throwing hand in his glove. The throwing arm is held stationary out in front of the body, then, with a flick of the wrist and forearm, the ball is tossed to the partner, who is 10 to 15 feet away. Work on mastering a perfect "striper."

One-Knee Striper Drill

Each player throws "stripers" while down on one knee. Partners are about 15 to 25 feet apart. This stresses upper-body mechanics including proper shoulder rotation and follow-through.

Standing Striper Drill

Throw a striper to a partner about 25 to 40 feet away. He throws a striper back. Play catch.

General Throwing Drills

Four Square

Split the team into four groups and place one group at each base, including home plate. The first player in line at the plate should have a ball which, on your command, he will throw to the first player in line at first base. After throwing the ball, he sprints to first and gets at the end of that line. The player who catches the ball at first throws it to the first player in line at second and the ball continues "around the horn." Each player sprints to the base to which he threw the ball and gets at the end of the line there. To execute this drill properly, all players must throw hard and run hard (sprint). Receivers of throws should give good targets. If a poor throw is made, the player who made the throw must retrieve the ball, and the coach tosses another ball into play quickly. Everyone must stay alert so that they are not hit with an errant throw.

Teach the players to turn "glove side" as they get set to throw to the next base. For example, the right-handed fielder at third who catches the ball will begin his turn to his left, toward left field, rather than to his right, toward home plate. He will pivot his body all the way around in a counterclockwise motion until he is facing home plate. This gets the body in a more natural throwing position and, with practice, becomes quite fluid.

Look-It-In Drill

This drill requires you to paint or draw stars, circles, diamonds, or other figures on softballs. Show these to your players and tell them that you will be hitting them ground balls and fly balls, which they are to field and throw to the base that you indicate. As they catch the ball and look it into the glove, they must, without delaying their throw, call out the figure etched on the ball. Draw enough figures in different locations on the surface of each softball so that players don't have to rotate the ball to hunt for the figure. Players should get in the habit of watching the ball *all the way* while playing catch, fielding grounders and flies, batting, even when taking a pitch (follow it right into the catcher's mitt).

Throw for Points

Have your players stand about 60 to 90 feet apart and throw to each other for accuracy. Use the following scoring system: Right at the chest = 5 points, head = 3 points, arms or legs = 1 point, any spot away from the body = −1 point. Fifty points wins the game. Set up an informal throwing tournament. For example, if you have 12 players on your team, pair them up, and throw for points. The six winners continue to compete until an eventual tournament throwing champ is determined. Use the eliminated players as "official scorers." Give the winner a striped softball or, better yet, give all the losers stripers so that they can work on their throwing at home.

Beat the Ball Drill

A baserunner takes off for first as if running out an inside-the-park home run. The coach hits a ground ball to an infielder, who must throw to first base. The first baseman throws to the catcher, who throws it back to the man who fielded the original ground ball. He returns it to the catcher, who starts the ball "around the horn" (first to second to third to home). Each fielder turns glove-side to throw to the next base. The final throw home must beat the baserunner who circles the bags. For lower levels of talent, change the drill so that there are fewer throws (e.g., the ground ball is fielded, thrown to first, and then sent around the horn). Any time the baserunner is between the two bases where a throw is being made, the two fielders involved must be on the same side of the runner to avoid hitting him with a throw.

IV Fielding

Good defensive qualities are quick hands and quick feet. With repetition, and emphasizing proper mechanics, quick hands and feet can be developed while honing defensive skills.

Glove Selection

Players should take as much care in selecting a glove as in selecting a bat. Many young players tend to choose gloves that are too large for them. Suggest that they try a small or medium-size one, which they can handle easily. It is a good idea to keep a softball in the glove when storing it between games and practices and during the off-season. Outfielders should select gloves with deep pockets and long, fly-ball-snaring fingers. Infielders should choose gloves with a flatter pocket and shorter fingers so that the ball doesn't "get lost" when they need to make a quick release. A youngster's glove should fit snugly on the hand and wrist to allow for control and quick reactions. Many players like to keep the index finger outside the glove but, for best control, teach your players to keep all their fingers within it.

Mental Aspects of Defensive Play

A good player must always know the number of outs, the score, the inning, and the bases occupied. He knows ahead of time what he will do if the ball is hit to him. Many of the best players *want* the ball hit to them, even in pressure situations. They have confidence in their ability to make the plays.

Defensive Mechanics

Fielders must get into a ready position as the ball is pitched. They need to be low and ready to move in any direction. We say, "Ya gotta be low and ready to go!" The feet must be slightly wider apart than the shoulders, with the knees bent and the weight leaning forward. We want our players to watch the pitched ball come off the bat.

FIGURE 4-1   **FIGURE 4-2**

FIELDING TECHNIQUE: *The fielder uses two hands and extends them well out in front of the body to "meet the ball."*

Infielders must always charge ground balls, especially slow rollers, "playing low" even when charging the ball. As they get set to field it, they must "break down" into proper fielding position. Many grounders must be handled in practices until youngsters get the feel for breaking down at the proper moment (many break down too late). In breakdown position, the feet should be shoulder width (or slightly more) apart, with the knees bent and the glove foot slightly in advance of the other foot. The hands must be well out in front of the body, with the thumbs pointing out, and the rear end must be down. The fielder should use both hands and extend them to meet the ball well out in front of his body. Keeping the glove low to the ground when approaching a grounder will make it less likely that the ball will go through the fielder's legs. Also, it is easier to come up with the glove quickly on a bad bounce than it is to go down on a ball that continues to roll. We tell our fielders to be alert and anticipate the unexpected: a bouncing ball may begin to roll and a rolling ball may bounce.

If you don't know a runner or batter, it is a good idea to assume that he has great speed. If the play is a double-play chance, make sure of the first out. Players should take their time and set up for the throw (feed) to second, thinking of the out at first only as a bonus. They should crow hop, and make a hard and accurate throw. Infielders should always dive at balls that are out of their normal reach. The primary object is to knock the ball down and keep it in the infield.

Getting a jump on the ball is just as important for infielders as it is for outfielders. We want our infielders to play deep with no one on base or with two outs, unless we anticipate a possible bunt. The deeper you play, the more ground you can cover. The coach must balance this universal truth with the threat of the bunt attempt in fast-pitch softball.

We find that young players, when going left or right for a ground ball that seems headed for a base hit, tend to follow the contour of the infield. They seem to think that they have to stay on the dirt infield. We teach them to angle back, running out onto the grass, if necessary, to get their hands on the ball. This may make for a longer throw, but at least the ball is being stopped before it gets to the outfield, which will prevent further advancement by other baserunners. For example, with a runner on second and a ball hit into the hole between third and short, the shortstop might angle back toward left field and field the ball. He may not have a play at first, or even third, but he can now hold the lead runner at third, keeping him from scoring on what would have been a clean hit to the outfield. And sometimes the lead runner can be caught off guard and gunned down at third after he has rounded the bag.

Many coaches are teaching their infielders to "circle the ball" or take a "banana route" toward the ball. Instead of charging directly at the ball, the idea is to loop to the right to get the body in a more direct line to first when the throw is made. With younger players you may find that, in trying this maneuver, they overdo it and run right by the ball, failing to stay in front of it. If so, postpone this technique until you feel that they are ready to implement it properly.

It is helpful to time your infielders to determine how long it takes each one to make a routine out, from the moment the ball hits the bat until his throw is caught by the first baseman. Also, time your runners from the time their bat hits the ball until they touch first. (Be sure to set the bases at 60 feet for fast-pitch softball and 65 feet for slow-pitch softball.) This data helps you select fielding positions suited to your players and lets them know how much time they have to make plays.

The Crossover Step

In going left or right to field a ball, players must execute a crossover step in the direction the ball was hit. When a ball is hit to a player's right, for example, he merely pivots on the balls of his feet and crosses his left foot over his right, keeping his glove low to the ground. A good dry drill to practice this technique is for the coach to

FIGURE 4-3

CROSSOVER STEP: *The fielder pivots on the balls of his feet, makes a crossover step while keeping his glove low, and completes the play.*

FIGURE 4-5

FIGURE 4-4

point right or left and have his players cross over in the appropriate direction, take three strides and get into breakdown position.

Combination Fielding and Throwing Drills

Catch with Two Hands

This drill drives home the importance of catching with two hands to get off a quicker throw. Send an equal number of players to home, first, second and third. The players at home and first are on the same team, as are the players at second and third. The first player at home plate and the first player at third base each have a ball and, on the coach's command, each throws it to the first player on his team at the opposite base. He then moves to the end of his own line. The player who catches the ball, using two hands, releases a quick throw back to the next player in the original line, and play continues until everyone has caught and thrown a ball. The team that finishes first wins. As an alternative to this, play catch for 30 or 60 seconds, and have the players count out loud the number of catches. Alternate catching with one hand and catching with two hands to emphasize the difference.

Wooden Gloves

Wooden gloves can help you teach your players to "give" with the ball and develop soft hands. The idea is to make gloves out of

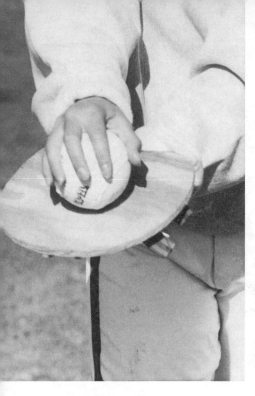

FIGURE 4-6
WOODEN GLOVE: *THe wooden glove teaches players to catch with two hands and to "give" with the ball as it is caught.*

plywood (see photo). The plywood glove is fastened to the hand by a rubber strap. It is impossible to field a ball with one hand and, since many balls are botched, it teaches players to stay with the ball, pounce on it, and pick it up with the bare hand to complete the play. Always follow a wooden glove session with a real glove session to transfer the skill from a drill to a more game-like situation.

Short Hop

Players pair up and throw short hops to each other. The ball must bounce on the ground slightly in front of the fielder's glove. The fielder keeps his feet stationary, bends his knees, and looks the ball into his glove. Next, take some backhand short hops. One player acts as tosser and gets down on one knee. Players switch on the coach's whistle or after a fixed number of short hops. It is important to remind players not to backhand the ball unless necessary. It is always preferable to get in front of the ball because a bad hop may bounce off your chest, stay in front of you, and allow you to still retire a baserunner.

Shadow Infield

This is a nifty way to get twice as many players into each play. Have a second player at each position about 12 feet behind the other.

FIGURE 4-7

FIGURE 4-8

SHORT HOP DRILL: *The tosser gets down on one knee and throws short hops to his partner. The fielder keeps his feet stationary, bends his knees, and looks the ball into the glove.*

FIGURE 4-9

The first player will field a ground ball and throw it to first, while the other acts as his shadow, charging the ball, breaking down, and making a crow hop and throw. As the second player is a kind of mirror image of the first, the coach can correct and instruct two players at once.

Three for You (or Four, or Five)

Hit three consecutive grounders to each fielder. They throw to first base, and as soon as they release the throw, the next ball is hit. This develops reflexes and getting a jump on the ball, and helps them develop a sense of where the bag is before they begin the throw to first.

Slow Rollers

The coach alternates hitting slow rollers to third, short, and second. Each infielder must charge it quickly and throw out a runner who takes off from home plate toward first as the ball is hit. Infielders must learn to charge hard, but slow down and come under control as they approach the ball. Use the pitchers, catchers, and outfielders as baserunners. Keep the runners "honest," as they tend to take off before the ball is hit and make things very difficult for the defense.

Look-'Em-Back

Use a line of runners at third and a line of runners at home. Hit ground balls to a drawn-in infield. As you hit the ball, the first runner in line at home takes off for first. The fielder should hold onto the ball, look the runner back to third and then throw to first. The runner at third can then try to score after the throw is made to first. After a player has run from third, he joins the line at home. After running from the plate to first, runners then move to the end of the line at third.

To practice game situations where the runner at third represents an important run, have your first baseman come off the bag toward the throw from third. He should then catch and throw the ball home for the out. Of course, the runner will be safe at first base, but the runner from third may be cut down at the plate.

V. Positional Play

The First Baseman

A good first baseman must be able to field, shift his feet quickly, and stretch for throws from infielders. Good size is an asset for a first sacker because he makes a large throwing target for infielders. Tall, lanky players have an obvious advantage in stretching ability and many coaches prefer a left-handed first baseman. A lefty can throw to the left side of the diamond without pivoting and, because his glove is on his right hand (in the direction of fair territory), he can field balls that righties would have to backhand.

There is no need to hold runners in fast-pitch or slow-pitch softball because they can't lead. In fast-pitch softball runners may leave the base when the pitch is released; in slow-pitch softball they can take off only when the ball reaches the plate. So, play your first baseman deep, unless you anticipate a possible bunt in fast-pitch games or an important run is at third with less than two outs (possible play at the plate).

When taking throws, the first baseman should face the throwing infielder, "heel" the bag, and give a chest-high target with both his glove hand and throwing hand. He shouldn't stretch until the ball is in flight toward him. Only then should he decide which foot will touch the bag and which will stretch toward the throw. If the throw is off to his left, he should shift left and touch the bag with the right foot. (To avoid being stepped on, he should touch the edge of the bag with the toe of his shoe.) If the throw is to the right, he can shift right and tag the bag with his left foot. For throws that are way off the mark, he should forget about getting an out, and come off the bag to catch the ball. This will prevent a wild throw from going out of the playing area, and keep the runner(s) from advancing further. Sometimes, a first baseman can come off the bag, catch an errant throw, and get back to the base in time to retire a runner (especially if the runner is slow and/or the ball is hit very hard).

A first sacker must try to block low throws with his body to keep them in front of him. This is a better strategy for youth softball than trying for the scoop or short hop, which often results in the throw going out of play and bases being awarded (you may want to work on

FIGURE 5-1

FIRST BASEMAN HEELS BAG:
The first baseman faces the
throwing infielder, "heeling" the
bag.

FIGURE 5-2

FIRST BASEMAN SHIFTS LEFT: If
the throw is off to her left, she
shifts left and touches the bag
with the right foot.

the "scoop" play with older players). For throws that are "right on the
money," a first baseman can touch the bag with either foot, and most
tend to stretch with the leg on their glove side.

If the throw comes from the direction of home plate (e.g., from the
catcher on a dropped third strike in fast-pitch softball), we want our
first baseman to set up so as to give the fielder the clearest shot at
retiring the runner. If the throw is coming from fair territory, he will
touch first with his left foot and give a target in fair territory, telling the
fielder to throw "Inside, Inside!" If the throw comes from foul territory,
he touches first with his right foot and gives a target in foul territory
calling "Outside, Outside!"

Sometimes, if an infielder loses control of a ground ball, he may
desperately continue his attempt to retire the runner. A good first
baseman must be able to size up the situation quickly. Does the
fielder still have a chance to get the runner? If so, he must make his
best stretch. If there is no chance to retire the runner and a hurried
attempt could result in a wild throw and further advance by the
runner(s), the first baseman should come off the bag toward the

FIGURE 5-3
FIRST BASEMAN SHIFTS RIGHT:
If the throw is off to her right, she shifts right and tags the bag with her left foot.

fielder, yelling "No! No! No!" and waving his arms. This is to prevent the fielder from going through with the play.

Finally, good baserunners are taught to "key" on the first baseman after hitting an infield ground ball. If the throw pulls the first baseman off the bag toward home, they are taught to slide to make it more difficult for them to be tagged out. A first baseman, then, should sweep tag *downward* in this situation.

First basemen need to work on fielding ground balls and throwing to the pitcher covering first. A pitcher should be prepared to cover first on any ball hit to the right side of the infield. Communication is crucial. On his way to cover first, the pitcher must listen to the first baseman, who might call out, "I'll take it myself!" The proper technique for pitchers and first basemen to execute this play is given in the "Pitcher as Infielder" section that follows. The first baseman should not be hesitant to go for ground balls hit to his right. The second baseman will call him off if he has a play on the ball and the pitcher will cover first if the first sacker can't get back to the bag. With practice, first sackers get a feel for what is their territory and what is in the second baseman's range.

Another important aspect of first-base play is the 3-6-3 double play. This is a "twin killing" started by a ground ball to the first baseman (whose fielding position is 3), who throws to the shortstop (6) covering second base, and gets back to first to take the return throw (3). Make sure your first sacker sets himself before making the throw to the shortstop. Hurried and off-balance throws are a leading cause of errors in softball. Sometimes the first baseman cannot get back to the bag in time to take the throw. By communicating, the pitcher and first baseman can work together on the 3-6-1 double play. Simply, the pitcher, or sometimes even the second baseman, will call out, "I have the throw!" The first baseman can acknowledge this with "Okay, you take it!" or "No! No! I've got it!"

Sometimes, with a runner on second (and less than two outs) and a ground ball to third or short, the runner takes off for third when the ball is thrown to first. If the runner headed for third represents an important run, you may want your first sacker to give up the out at first, come off the bag toward the ball, catch it, and throw to third to nail the big run. A similar situation sometimes occurs with a runner on third and a ground ball to the left side. The defensive play described is a gamble, but if you pull it off, your team will look like a heads-up, well-coached unit. And to pull it off in games, you have to practice it.

Note: Bunt coverage in fast-pitch softball and cut-offs are handled in Chapter X.

The Third Baseman

The third baseman must have a strong arm and be able to range far to his left. He must be quick and aggressive and have the guts to stay down in front of hard-hit balls. In fast-pitch softball, he should always be alert for possible bunt situations. He shouldn't hesitate or pull up short on balls hit toward short. The shortstop will call him off if he feels that he as a better play than the third sacker. Third basemen can't be afraid to "play horizontal." They should dive to knock down drives, especially those hit to their right, which could end up as two-base hits.

The third baseman doesn't have to be as sure-handed as the middle infielders (second baseman and shortstop). Often he is able to knock down a ground ball, pounce on it, and still have time to throw out a runner. A good drill to teach this involves having your third baseman wear a catcher's mask or even full catcher's gear (including supporter and protective cup for males) while taking grounders. The third baseman must place his hands behind his back and knock the ball down with his chest. Coaches should hit medium-velocity grounders and the third baseman should try to stay square to the plate as he attempts to block the ball with his body. Once he knocks the ball down, he may use his hands to complete the play.

FIGURE 5-4

FIGURE 5-5

TWO WAYS OF PICKING UP A STOPPED BALL WITH THE BARE HAND: The fielder may secure a good grip by pushing the ball into the ground with the fingers pointed down, or he may scoop it up with the fingers beneath. Younger players and those with small hands may prefer the latter technique.

Third basemen in both fast- and slow-pitch softball must work on charging slow rollers (bunts and "swinging bunts"). If the ball is rolling, we want our fielders to use two hands fielding it. If it has stopped, we prefer them to pick it up with the throwing hand and release a quick, sidearm throw. In either case, they should not take their eyes off a slow roller until it is held securely in hand. There are two methods for picking up a stopped ball with the bare hand. One is to secure a good grip by pushing it into the ground with the fingers pointed downward. The other is to scoop it up with the fingers underneath it. Younger players and those with small hands may prefer the latter technique.

An effective slow-roller drill involves lining three softballs about 10 feet apart in fair territory down the third baseline, each one 10 feet closer to home than the one before. The third baseman must charge the first ball, pick it up, and throw to first, then immediately play the second and the third softballs in the same manner. He might play all with two hands or all with one hand. Or he might field the first with two hands and the final two with one hand.

The Middle Infielders

The middle infielders must be your most sure-handed, smooth-fielding, and wide-ranging fielders. They must have quickness as well as speed, agility, and a quick throwing release.

Shortstop Feeds

A "feed" is a throw that starts a double play. The fielder is feeding a teammate a good throw so that he can make a quick pivot. The shortstop makes a different feed, depending on where he fields the ball. First off, if he fields it close to second base he should make no feed at all, but yell, "I'll take it!" to tell his second baseman to get out of the way, then make the double-play pivot and throw himself. If the ground ball is close to second, but not close enough for the shortstop to take it himself, he should make an underhand, chest-high toss to the second baseman. When making this feed it is best to keep the hands well separated. He should take the ball out of the glove and show it clearly to the pivot man rather than toss it with his throwing hand still in the glove area. This makes it easier for the second sacker to pick up the flight of the ball.

If the ground ball is hit directly at the shortstop, he should pivot on the balls of both feet so that his toes point toward second, and then release an overhand throw. If the grounder is to his right, he should field the ball, stay low, and make a sidearm throw to the bag. If it is

FIGURE 5-6

FIGURE 5-7

FIGURE 5-8

SLOW-ROLLER DRILL: Line three softballs about 10 feet apart in fair territory down the third base line. The third baseman charges the first ball, picks it up, and throws to first. Immediately he plays the second and third softballs in the same manner.

FIGURE 5-9
**SHORTSTOP UNDERHAND
FEED:** *The shortstop makes an
underhand, chest high toss,
keeping his hands well separated
to give the second baseman a
clear view of the ball.*

FIGURE 5-10
SHORTSTOP FEED: *The shortstop
pivots on the balls of both feet so
that his toes point toward second
and then releases an overhand
throw.*

well to his right, he may have to stand up and fire an overhand strike
to second. Finally, if the ball is behind second base, he might have to
make a backhand toss.

Second Baseman Feeds

For ground balls fielded very close to second, the second baseman should take it himself, following the same technique as the
shortstop. Similarly, if the ball is too far away from the bag for the
second baseman to take himself, he should make an underhand,
chest-high feed to the shortstop covering second. For grounders
right at him, he can pivot his upper body, pointing his toes toward
second, and toss overhand. If the ball is fielded close to the baseline
and within about 20 feet of the bag, the second baseman should
make a backhand flip (see photo). If he goes to his left to field the
ball, he must shift his feet so that he is facing second, and then throw.
For balls fielded well to his left and out toward right field, the second

FIGURE 5-11

FIGURE 5-12

SHORTSTOP SIDEARM FEED: *The shortstop stays low and makes a sidearm throw to the bag.*
FIGURE 5-13

SECOND BASEMAN FEED: The second baseman pivots his upper body, pointing his toes toward second, and tosses overhand.

FIGURE 5-14

FIGURE 5-15

SECOND BASEMAN BACKHAND FLIP: The second baseman stays low and flips the ball to the shortstop with a backhand motion.

baseman should turn counterclockwise (toward center field), set, and fire a strike to second.

Double-Play Pivots

How a double-play pivot is made depends on where the ball was hit, how much time is available, and the position of a sliding runner. Make sure your players get an out, the double play being a bonus. The shortstop's basic pivot is a drag step. He sets up behind the bag facing the fielder (first or second baseman) who will make the throw. He steps to the left of and parallel to second with his left foot, catches the feed with two hands, and drags his right foot across the bag as he gets off a strong throw to first. This pivot should take him a full stride in the direction of right field and away from the sliding runner. If the feed is late, he should step on the back of the bag with his left foot

SHORTSTOP DRAG STEP: *If the feed is early, the shortstop should step toward first base and drag his rear foot across the base as he throws to first base.*

FIGURE 5-16

SHORTSTOP LATE THROW PIVOT: *If the feed is late, the shortstop should step on the back of the bag with his left foot and throw from behind the base to avoid a sliding runner.*

FIGURE 5-17

FIGURE 5-18

FIGURE 5-19

FIGURE 5-20

SHORTSTOP INSIDE PIVOT: *If the feed is to the inside of the diamond, the shortstop should step on the inside corner of second base with his left foot. He should catch the ball with two hands and push off the bag toward the pitcher's plate. Landing on his right foot, he should step toward first with his left foot and throw to first.*

FIGURE 5-21

FIGURE 5-22

FIGURE 5-23

SECOND BASEMAN PIVOT: *The basic pivot for second baseman is to hit the bag with the left foot and bounce back away from it, getting off a strong throw.*

FIGURE 5-24

FIGURE 5-25

SECOND BASEMAN DRAG STEP: *The second baseman steps to the inside of the bag with the left foot. He executes a drag step across the bag with the right foot. Planting the right foot hard, he throws to first.*

FIGURE 5-26

and throw from behind the base to avoid a sliding runner. If the feed is to the inside of the diamond, the shortstop should use an "inside pivot." He steps on the inside corner of second base with his left foot, catches the ball with two hands, and pushes off the bag toward the pitcher's plate. Landing on his right foot, he steps toward first with his left foot, and throws to first.

The basic pivot for second basemen is to hit the bag with the left foot and bounce back away from it, getting off a strong throw. The second baseman should set up with both feet behind the bag (toward right field). He takes the feed with two hands, tags the bag with the left foot, and pushes off *backward* toward right field. If the throw is left or right, he can shift his feet like a first baseman, tag the bag, and throw to first. Another popular pivot is the drag step. He steps to the inside of the bag with the left foot and does a drag step across the bag with the right foot, then plants it hard while throwing to first.

The Pitcher as Infielder

A pitcher becomes an infielder as soon as he releases each pitch. His follow-through, then, should leave him in a good defensive position, ready to field a ball batted in any direction. He should end up with both feet parallel to each other and with the glove waist-high in front of him.

A good drill to work on fielding with your pitchers is to have them line up at the pitcher's plate and take turns delivering a pitch to the catcher. As the pitch reaches the plate, the coach should fungo a ground ball right back to the pitcher who fields it and throws to first. This is also a good way to work on the pitcher starting the 1-6-3 double play. After fielding the ball, he can either make a throw that leads the shortstop (or second baseman—the pitcher must know who will be taking the throw on this potential double play *before* he pitches the ball) to the bag, or wait until the shortstop is set. Generally, be sure of one out. Don't rush. By the time the pitcher fields the ball, the batter is barely out of the batter's box. With runners on first and third, you may want your pitchers to fake the runner at third back to the bag and then start the double play.

Pitchers must be prepared to cover first on any ball that is hit to the right side of the infield. On any ball batted to his left, then, a pitcher should sprint to a point about 10 feet down the line in front of first base. Taking short choppy strides when nearing the bag will make it easier for him to adjust to a poor throw from the first sacker. The first baseman should try to get the ball to the pitcher a few steps before the bag so that he can catch it and still have time to look for, and tag, the bag. If possible, we like our first baseman to be moving toward

FIGURE 5-27

PITCHER COVERING FIRST: *The pitcher sprints to a point about 10 feet down the line in front of first base and begins running parallel to the baseline. The first baseman tries to get her the ball a few steps before*

first while making an underhand toss to the pitcher. This shortens the throw and gets momentum moving in that direction. Pitchers should try to catch the ball with two hands, step on the inside of the bag, and veer in toward second base to avoid the batter-baserunner. If the pitcher arrives at first early, he should set up and "heel" the bag like a first baseman.

In slow-pitch softball, the pitcher generally backs up toward second after each delivery (see Chapter VIII). There is a trade-off here that each pitcher must consider for himself. The farther he backs up after pitching, the more ground he can cover up the middle, but the farther away he takes himself from first.

Youth softball always generates a great many wild pitches and passed balls (to alleviate the problem, some leagues don't allow runners to advance on these). Practice having the pitcher cover home, take a throw from the catcher, and make a quick tag. As the pitcher charges home, he should stop in front of the plate to give the runner a clear shot at home (to encourage him to slide and to avoid a collision). Ideally, the pitcher will receive a knee-high throw and quickly drop the glove down along the third-base side of the plate, letting the sliding runner, in effect, tag himself out.

FIGURE 5-28

the bag so that she can catch it and still have time to look for and tag the bag.

FIGURE 5-29

The Catcher

Having a good defensive catcher is much more important in fast-pitch than in slow-pitch softball. Since in slow-pitch softball there is no bunting, and no advancing on passed balls, wild pitches, and dropped third strikes, many teams "hide" a weak fielder at the catching position. The ball is "dead" (no players may advance) in the slow-pitch game as soon as a pitch hits the ground (while in fast-pitch the batter *may* hit a pitch on the bounce), so in many games the slow-pitch catcher does little more than catch the ball and return it to his pitcher.

As in fast-pitch softball, the slow-pitch catcher should run down and back up first on ground balls to the infield whenever no one is on base or only first is occupied. In doing this, he should angle back about 30 feet or more into foul territory, if the field dimensions allow it. If he gets too close to first, any ball that gets past the first baseman is likely to get past him, too. The slow-pitch catcher should try to catch each pitch with his glove on the ground, letting the ball come down so that the umpire can follow the entire path of the pitch. Rather than sitting back on his haunches or on one knee, as many catches do, he should be alert and ready to move quickly. He may have to field "swinging bunts" or foul pops, and may have to cover home on force plays or tag plays (see below).

Developing a good working relationship with the plate umpire, a smart catcher can help his pitcher by relaying information about why certain pitches are not strikes (deep, hit the plate, inside, etc.). He can also be a team leader by keeping everybody heads-up. Before each batter steps up to the plate, he can help position his teammates and inform them of the number of outs and where possible plays can be made. He also must line up infielders for cut-offs (see Chapter X for relay and cut-off drills).

A good play that often works for both the fast-pitch and slow-pitch catcher is to follow the batter to first on a hit to right field. If the first baseman moves toward the outfield (where the runner sees him and thinks that first is unguarded), the catcher may be able to sneak in behind and receive a quick throw from the outfielder, picking off the unsuspecting batter-baserunner. Try this play when there are no other baserunners to worry about, and be alert to the possibility of the batter-baserunner taking off for second as the throw comes in to first. If he does take off, the catcher must move toward the throw to get his hands on the ball as soon as possible, and then throw a quick strike to second.

The Fast-pitch Catcher

The fast-pitch catcher must be quick and agile, with a strong and accurate throwing arm (though we feel that a quick release is even more important than a strong arm). Good size and upper-body strength can only help a catcher who often has to block a speedy runner from the plate. We are especially fond of catchers with a "take charge" attitude. Finally, the ability to handle pitchers is an important skill, because a pitcher's mental condition greatly influences his performance. A catcher must be alert to any change in his pitcher's "stuff," control, or mental state, and react accordingly. A catcher who instills confidence and can help steady a struggling pitcher is a valuable asset to a team.

The catcher must give signals to his pitcher but make sure that the opponents don't see them. Most teams use a simple digit system with, say, one finger for a fastball, two for a rise, and three for a change-up. The catcher usually sits back on his heels and gives signals from the crotch area, with his knees close enough to shield his signals from the base coaches' view. He can place his glove alongside his left knee to further restrict the third-base coach's view (see photo). We feel that pitchers should throw whatever pitch the catcher calls rather than shake off pitches. Coaches should teach their catchers how they want them to call a game, and then let each catcher do his job. If a coach feels it necessary, he can relay signals to the catcher to call a particular pitch at any given time.

Catcher's Stance

Most catchers get set up too far back in the catcher's box, afraid of interfering with, or being hit by, the bat. Being too far back means more balls in the dirt and fewer foul tips caught. If also makes the umpire's job tougher and your pitcher may not get some strike calls that he deserves. For example, a moving pitch that was on the outside corner as it crossed the plate may be six inches outside by the time the deep catcher snares it. Get your catcher up close where he can keep those pitches in the strike zone. A rule of thumb is to get him close enough to the batter so that he can reach up and touch him with his mitt. Also, teach him not to catch the ball close to his body, but to meet the ball as close to the plate as he can without interfering with the batter.

With no one on base, a catcher doesn't have to worry about balls in the dirt unless the hitter gets two strikes, which makes possible a dropped third strike. But *any time* a ball gets through to the backstop, it tends to shake up the pitcher, and his mental state is critical, so we want our catchers to try to block every pitch in the dirt, regardless of the situation. They need the practice anyway!

Though many coaches will let their catchers get down on one knee when there are no baserunners, we want our catchers to get into the same crouch position always. The elbows should be outside the knees, the feet slightly wider than the shoulders (most catchers

FIGURE 5-30

CATCHER'S STANCE: *Proper catcher's stance*

FIGURE 5-31

CATCHER'S SIGNALS: *Note catcher's mitt positioned to hide signals from third base coach.*

place the left foot slightly ahead of the right), and the body weight on the balls of the feet. The rear end should not be too low and the back should be nearly flat. Our catchers get set early and give the pitcher a consistent, stationary target. Generally, the target (glove) is held low (fingers pointing up) and the catcher should stay down in front of the umpire to give him the best possible view of the strike zone. Many coaches prefer the catcher to keep his throwing hand behind his back for safety. Others allow this with no runners on base, but otherwise insist that two hands be used to insure a quick throwing release. Either way, make sure the catcher tucks his throwing hand thumb under the fingers for protection against foul balls—though he should not clench his fist tightly.

Framing (catching and keeping pitches in the strike zone) is a vital skill for fast-pitch catchers. Too many young catchers "butcher the strike zone." When catching a ball near the batter's armpits, for example, they lunge upward or sometimes even stand up, carrying the ball well out of the strike zone. Similarly, they inadvertently carry low pitches as well as inside and outside pitches away from the strike zone, making them look like obvious balls rather than borderline strikes. With practice and correct use of framing technique, a catcher

FIGURE 5-32

FRAMING INSIDE PITCH: *The catcher rotates his glove hand so that his thumb turns toward his body, keeping the inside pitch over the strike zone.*

FIGURE 5-33

FRAMING HIGH PITCH: *Catcher points the glove hand fingers down slightly keeping the high strike in the strike zone.*

can keep close pitches within the strike zone and give the umpire a good look at them.

Let's assume there is a right-handed batter up and a right-handed catcher. For pitches on the inside part of the plate, the catcher should keep his mitt stationary over the inside corner and rotate his glove hand about 45 degrees so that his thumb turns toward his body. This allows the catch to be made and keeps the catcher from reaching out to catch the ball and carrying it away from the plate in the process. For outside pitches, he should try to meet the ball near the plate and hold the glove steady so that the ball remains on the outside corner— not lunge after it and push it toward the first-base dugout area. For high pitches, he should point the glove hand fingers down slightly so that the ball does not appear higher than it actually is. On low pitches, he should keep the fingers pointed up, if possible. If he has to point his fingers toward the ground, he should rotate the glove slightly upward to keep the ball near the hitter's knees. Many catchers like to sway on the balls of their feet when framing inside and outside pitches. When they sway slightly, rather than move the feet and body,

FIGURE 5-34
FRAMING LOW PITCH: *Fingers up.*

FIGURE 5-35
FRAMING LOW PITCH: *Fingers down*

it becomes more obvious to the umpire that the ball stayed in the strike zone.

Blocking Pitches in the Dirt

The fast-pitch catcher must be well schooled in blocking balls in the dirt. As a youth coach, you will probably find that there are as many (or more) passed balls in your games as there are errors. The catcher must go to his knees to block low pitches. He cannot scoop or short-hop them or flail helplessly at them with his glove. He must drop down and drive both knees forward with his elbows locked and his glove perpendicular to the ground. Keeping his throwing hand behind the mitt with his thumb protected as described above, he must tuck in his chin, move forward, and smother the ball, ensuring that his mitt is on the ground, so that a ball cannot pass under it and between his legs. Also, he must try to remain square to the pitcher so that any ball that bounces off his chest will stay in front of him, rather than bounce off to the sidelines.

A good first drill to teach blocking technique is to get a young catcher set up with full catching gear and on his knees in blocking position. From this position, have him block (not necessarily catch) balls that you throw at him from 25 or 30 feet away. Throw directly at him and about a foot or more in front of him. Teach him to keep the chin tucked, the throwing hand protected behind the mitt, and the eyes looking straight at the ball. If he turns his head, he not only loses sight of the ball, but the protection of the mask as well. Next, get him in his catching position and have him drop down on both knees when you throw balls in the dirt. Finally, throw low pitches to his right and left that he must block, "squaring up" to the pitcher. If the ball is to his right, he drops to the right knee first, quickly bringing the other leg into blocking position. If the ball is to his left, he drops his left knee first and quickly follows with the right. You may want to use tennis balls or whiffle balls for these drills to prevent injury.

Dry blocking is a useful practice mode. The coach gets in front of the catcher and points to where an imaginary ball has bounced and the catcher (in full gear) must react accordingly. A variation on this is to put three balls down in different positions in front of the catcher (one to his right, one directly in front, and one to his left), and have him go from one to the next, dropping into blocking position and back into catching position.

Another good drill puts your catchers in full gear at third base or shortstop. Hit ground balls and have them go down to both knees and block them in the dirt. You may want to protect throwing hands by using boxing gloves or just hit tennis balls or whiffle balls. There is a trade-off with the safer balls: They protect the catcher but produce less realistic play.

FIGURE 5-36

CATCHER BLOCKING BALL IN DIRT: *Elbows are locked and the glove is perpendicular to and touching the ground. The chin is tucked, the throwing hand is protected, and the body is square to the pitcher.*

Throwing Out Stealing Runners

Throwing out stealing runners requires quick and accurate throws. A strong arm is a plus, but the quick release is critical. When readying to throw, the catcher must bring the throwing hand behind the glove (foul tips go up or down, so this is a reasonably safe position). He should throw overhand while stepping toward the target with his guide shoulder and hip pointing toward it.

It is important to learn the proper footwork for throwing out runners. The catcher actually starts his footwork *before* he catches the ball. As the pitch is delivered and a steal is in progress, the catcher must step forward with his right foot. Coaches call this a jab step, and it is made just before the ball is caught. Next, the left foot steps toward second and the throw is made. The catcher must try to stay low during his throws, as time is wasted while standing up. You may want to have very young catchers crow hop and throw so that they can reach second (but don't allow several steps to be taken before the crow hop). However young the player, always emphasize quickness of release and accuracy over velocity.

Most catchers react quickly to recover a passed ball but then waste time looking to see if the runner is advancing. By the time they go into their throwing motion, it is too late to retire the runner. A catcher should pounce on the ball, turn to begin throwing to cut down the runner, and *abort the throw if he sees he has no play*, or if his teammates call out, "No Play! No Play!"

Two catchers can practice at once throwing to second by setting up two groups of three (catcher, pitcher and second baseman). Station each catcher behind home plate on either side of it, and each pitcher on either side of the pitcher's plate. Place two movable bags on each side of second base, but far enough apart so that errant throws don't enter the other second baseman's area. Keep a straight line between each catcher, pitcher, and second baseman. Catchers work on a quick release and accurate, knee-high throws. Pitchers work on the pitch-out or spot pitching. Second basemen work on taking throws and making good tags.

When throwing to third, the catcher should place his right foot behind his left to avoid the right-handed batter before getting off his throw. The catcher's throwing footwork takes a great deal of practice, but with repetition the movements become automatic.

Catching Foul Pops

Foul flies to the catcher come down with a spin that brings them in toward the diamond. Because of this, the catcher should always face the backstop when fielding a high pop-up. He will find it easier facing this way and letting the ball drift in to him, rather than facing the

FIGURE 5-37

FIGURE 5-38

FIGURE 5-39

CATCHER THROWS TO SECOND:
The catcher jabs with his right foot before the ball is caught. The left foot steps toward second and the throw is made.

infield and chasing a ball that is moving away from him. He should catch the ball with his glove up above his head like any other infielder. The catcher should take off his mask but not throw it until he has a bead on the ball. Only then should he toss it *away from where he will be making the play.* If he tosses the mask without gauging the flight of the ball, he may find himself drifting over to where he tossed it, then stumbling over it.

High pops tend to drift in toward the infield, so the catcher should go to the backstop even on flies that appear to be out of the playing field. High foul pops are very tough plays for catchers. Therefore, the catcher should have last priority (especially for pop-ups in or near fair territory), and readily give way to the first baseman or third baseman, if they call for the ball. Even the pitcher generally has an easier play then the catcher.

To practice these, the coach must be able to hit high pop-ups, as throwing them will not impart the same spin to the ball. With a little practice, any coach who can hit fungoes reasonably well can learn to fungo high pops, too. When working on foul pops, put the infielders (and outfielders, if you like) in their positions as well, so that flies that are not fungoed exactly right can be fielded by them, and make sure your catchers use full gear. Always make practice conditions as game-like as possible.

Fielding Bunts

The fast-pitch catcher must field bunts, and both fast-pitch and slow-pitch catchers must handle "swinging bunts." The catcher should scoop the ball with both hands, using the glove and bare hand in a sweeping motion as if using a dustpan and brush. He should never pick up the ball with the mitt alone. If the ball is batted near the first base line, he should take a step back away from the foul line before throwing to first, to reduce the chance of hitting the batter-baserunner. If the ball is out in front of the plate, he should *circle* the ball, as described earlier in this chapter, to get into a better position to throw to first. Finally, if the ball is fielded by the catcher down the third base line, he should turn glove-side to throw to first.

Tagging Out Runners at the Plate

Throwing out a runner at home plate provides a great psychological boost to a team's morale. Good teams need to make this play whenever possible, while insuring that the catcher doesn't get hurt in the process. As the throw comes in from the outfielder, the catcher should square up to the direction of the throw and place his left foot on the front edge of the plate. This allows the runner to see the plate

FIGURE 5-40

FIGURE 5-41

FIGURE 5-42

CATCHER BLOCKING PLATE: *The catcher squares up to the direction of the throw placing his left foot on the front edge of the plate. If the throw is on target and in time to retire the runner, he steps in front of the plate with his left foot and shin guard pointing toward the runner. He stays low, making the tag with both hands.*

FIGURE 5-43

BULLFIGHTER'S TAG: *The catcher tags the runner and quickly spins away from any contact.*

(the catcher cannot block it legally unless he has the ball). Being given a clear view of home plate encourages runners to slide, and, with the catcher in front, he is likely to slide toward the back side of the plate. (There is much less chance of injury to the catcher if the runner slides.) If the throw comes in on target and with time to spare, the catcher may block the plate. To do this he should step in front of the plate with his left foot and shin guard pointing toward the runner. He must stay down, keeping his center of gravity low. He should make the tag with both hands, wrapping the entire throwing hand inside the mitt to prevent dropping the ball. After making the tag, he should roll with the impact and, like any fielder making a tag, bounce around to check the position of any other runner(s). If the throw is short, the catcher must decide whether to take the throw on the short hop or to go out to meet the ball and then come back to make the tag. If he thinks the runner will be safe at home, he definitely should meet the short throw and check the other runner(s). On a close tag play at any base, players have a tendency to start to tag the runner *before they have control of the ball.* They also tend to look at the runner before they have the ball, and, in both cases, they fail to catch it. They must concentrate on completing the catch first, then making the tag.

FIGURE 5-44
FIGURE 5-45

Any time the runner stays on his feet, the catcher should make a "bullfighter's tag," that is, tag the runner and quickly spin away from any contact like a matador. Avoid a collision whenever possible, as the speeding runner has momentum on his side. For safety's sake, we recommend that catchers stay in full gear (including mask) when making tag plays at the plate. If they complain that the mask tends to hamper their vision, tell them "So does a collision with a speeding runner." They are able to catch fastballs pitched from 35 to 46 feet away with no problem looking through the mask, so they should be able to catch a ball thrown from the outfield. The only time we concede that vision is impaired by peering through the bars of the catcher's mask is during a high pop-up. Catchers should keep the mask on at all other times.

In A.S.A. softball, when the catcher misses the tag *and* the runner misses home plate, the umpire will make a safe sign. There are two reasons for this. One is that the umpire doesn't want to tip either team off that something is wrong, and by making no sign he would indeed be indicating this. The other reason is that a runner is considered to have touched a base that he passes until such time that the defense appeals the play. So, in fact, he *is* safe—so far. To appeal, have your catcher tag the runner, if he is still in the field of play (don't go into the dugout after him), or step on the plate and say "Ump, the runner who just scored missed home." (See Appendix F for more on appeal plays.)

Outfield Play

Outfield play is probably the most neglected and least efficient part of softball practice. Coaches tend to think that a good outfielder is one who can catch fly balls. Consequently, they hit their outfielders one routine fly ball after another during practices. If a player can't catch the routiners by the time he is 14 or 15 years old, he should find a new position or a new sport. The truth is that catching fly balls is only a tiny part of becoming a good outfielder. The marks of a quality outfielder are how quickly he can judge a fly ball and "get a jump on it," how much ground he can cover, how well he can *go back* for a drive, how well he can field base hits, how well he throws, and how well he backs up bases in game situations. Except for throwing, these facets are quite generally overlooked in many softball practices.

Outfielders must be alert to field conditions at various parks and weather conditions on different days. Will the ball bounce high because of dry, hard ground, or will it plop into mud? Is the grass moist? Softballs tend to skip off wet grass. If there is an outfield fence, what kind is it and how is the ball likely to carom off it? Smart players adjust to varying weather conditions. Indeed, it is a good idea to practice outfield play on some of the worst weather days (very bright sunshine, high winds, wet grounds).

Look for speed when choosing your outfielders, with the center-fielder usually being the fastest and the surest defensive player. All outfielders should be ready to move into action on every pitch. They should be "low and ready to go" and in the athletic position described in Chapter II. Once in motion, an outfielder should run on the balls of his feet to help keep his eyes from jarring with each stride. Too many outfielders run lazily after flies, arriving where the ball is headed just as it gets there. We want our outfielders to sprint to the spot where the ball will come down and *be there waiting for it*. They should catch with two hands (the thumb of the throwing hand overlaps the thumb of the glove hand), holding the glove toward the throwing shoulder to make for a quicker release. Outfielders should always assume that a ground ball will get through the infielder, even if it is right at an infielder, so they should begin sprinting toward the ground ball at the instant it is hit. Moreover, on every play an outfielder must be moving somewhere to make a play or to back up a base. Make your outfielders active participants, not spectators.

We want our outfielders to throw overhand, low, and hard. We like them to crow hop and release the ball with a strong wrist snap. One-hop throws to any base are acceptable, even desirable, and are often easy for infielders to handle. A low throw will get there quicker than a high one and any bounce will be low, cover more distance, and reach the infielder's knees or waist.

Your outfielders (and other players) must learn the art of communicating while playing ball. An outfielder, for example, can help a fellow outfielder by shouting "Back! Back! Back!" to warn him to go back on the ball, or "In, In, In!" to get him charging a soft liner. Train your infielders to go for a pop-up until they hear an outfielder call for it, and then give way to the outfielder immediately. (There is more on pop-up and fly-ball communication in Chapter IX.)

Drills to Improve Outfield Play

Note: Many fungo hitters prefer to hit to outfielders from out beyond the pitcher's plate rather than from the home plate area.

Two-Ball

This is an important drill to help outfielders learn to get a jump on the ball. Put half your outfielders in left field and half in right. You will have two fungo hitters hitting simultaneously (each has a shagger). The fungo hitters hit fly balls to the first left fielder and the first right fielder, who make the catch and throw the ball immediately to the appropriate shagger. As soon as the outfielder *releases the throw* to the shagger, a second ball is fungoed and the fielder must react quickly, gauge the ball's trajectory, get the quickest possible jump, and complete the catch. After making the second catch, the outfielder throws the ball to the shagger and goes to the end of his line. This drill is so important to an outfielder's skill development that it cannot be done too often. A variation of this is the three-ball drill, which uses three softballs instead of two.

Range

Put a line of outfielders in left centerfield and another in right centerfield. Each line has its own hitter and shagger. The fungo hitter for the left centerfielders hits a fly to the first player. It should be a high drive toward the left field line. After the fielder makes the play and returns the ball to the shagger, he stays on the left field line until the other members of his line have fielded a drive and lined up behind him. Similarly, the fungo hitter for the right centerfielders hits flies toward the right field line, making the fielders cover as much ground as possible. The right centerfielders, after making their plays, also line up on the right field line. After every player in a line makes it to the foul line, the fungo hitter starts hitting drives back toward the fielders' original location. The drill continues in this manner, giving players practice ranging far to their left and right.

Make sure that your players don't run with the glove outstretched, as this slows them down. Teach them to extend the glove at the last moment, and encourage them to make an attempt on every play. Too many players run "a mile" for the ball, then, thinking they have no play, watch it fall to the ground. Tell them, as we do, to give it a shot—leap, dive, at least stick their glove out. Sometimes, a great fielding play only requires a fielder who will make a great effort.

Liner

Use three lines of outfielders, one each in left field, centerfield, and right field. Each line has its own fungo hitter and shagger. Try to hit low, hard liners right at the fielder as well as to his left and right. Each player takes a turn and then gets at the end of his line. Hard-hit liners tend to rise, so make sure players stay back on the ball.

Shallow

This is the same as the Liner Drill, except that you have all fielders play in 10 to 15 steps and hit the ball over their heads—both liners and high drives. This is a critical drill because an outfielder who can go back well can play shallow, and may be able to turn many sure-fire base hits into outs. (Players shouldn't overdo it, though, because when they get burned, it will be for extra bases.) Don't let your players backpedal. Make them turn and sprint to catch long flies.

A word about going back on the ball: When a drive is hit almost directly over a fielder's head, he must turn either to his right or left as he begins the chase. We find that the fielder tends not to run straight back for the ball, but slightly in the direction that he turned. Because of this, after a long run, he may find that the ball ends up on the other side of his body. If he still has a play, it is now a difficult, sometimes off-balanced attempt. Players often say, mistakenly, "I turned the wrong way," when this occurs. Teach your players that turning the wrong way is not the problem, but that they must concentrate on going *straight back* for the ball.

Angle-Back

How many times have you watched helplessly as your left fielder and centerfielder chased a line-drive base hit and the ball skipped neatly between them? The hit goes for extra bases, sometimes even as inside-the-park home run. This hit becomes a "tweener" because outfielders don't angle back to field a gapper. The savvy outfielder learns to angle his run back to deeper territory rather than sprint straight across the field toward the ball. He gauges at what point on the field he can cut the ball off, then sprints to that spot. There is a drill to perfect this technique:

Use the same set-up and format as the Range Drill and add a cut-off man for each line. This time, instead of high drives, hit hard base hits that require the fielders to angle back to head them off. The cut-off man goes out into the outfield after the ball is hit, waves his arms, and yells, "Hit me! Hit me!", giving the outfielder a throwing target. Fielders try to make strong, accurate throws, hitting the cut-off man in the chest.

Do Or Die

Place your outfielders in their regular positions. Alternate hitting each fielder hard base hits. But before hitting the ball, yell out either "Do Or Die!" or "Regular!" *Do Or Die* tells the outfielder that the winning run is about to be scored on this hit. He must charge the ball, scoop it on the run, and fire a low, hard strike to home plate to save the game (retiring an imaginary runner from second). *Regular*, however, means that this is a "regular" base hit with no one on base. The fielder should charge the ball more cautiously, get down on one knee, if necessary, to block the ball, then throw low and hard to second base to hold the imaginary batter-baserunner at first.

Keep this drill moving or you will end up with players standing around waiting for the next play. As soon as one outfielder makes this throw, get the next ball in play. This will keep everybody alert and ready as balls are constantly being batted to left, right, and center. (Note: Additional fielding drills—including an important pop-up and fly ball communication drill and proper run-down procedure—are included in Chapter IX.)

VI. BASERUNNING

Baserunning practice is often neglected by coaches, and this is a big mistake. Intelligent, daring baserunning makes for a winning team and an exciting game to watch. Alert, aggressive baserunning keeps the pressure on the defense, and leads to more errors on their part and more runs on yours. Fielders defending against aggressive baserunning teams make more errors because they tend to rush, to look up before they have control of the ball, and to make hurried and off-balance throws.

When selecting players for your team, never underestimate the importance of speed. Speed helps a team on defense as well as offense. Although speed is a tremendous asset, a player can be an excellent baserunner without it. Sound baserunning instincts, quickness, and the ability to make good, quick decisions can compensate for lack of speed. Note the difference between speed and quickness. Speed is a measure of how fast a player can get from one place to another; quickness is a measure of how fast he can start, stop, and change directions.

The Importance of First- and Third-Base Coaches

We try never to allow a player to coach third base, preferring an adult there, unless this is forbidden by league rules. The third-base coach is an extremely important cog in the offensive machine. He must be alert at all times, and thinking ahead about what plays may possibly develop. "What will I likely do on a base hit with Sue on second? Which outfielders have strong, accurate arms? How should the score, inning, number of outs, and other factors affect my decision?" The third-base coach must never be caught off guard when he has to make a quick decision whether or not to send a runner. We feel that all of this is too much for a youth player to handle, which is why we prefer an adult third-base coach. Although first-base coaching is important too, it is not nearly as critical, and we permit alert youths to coach there. We recommend using baserunning coaches in your baserunning practice drills. Whether or not your players will be coaching bases during games, give them experience in practice.

It is smart (but seldom used) technique for the third-base coach to leave his coaching box and move down the line toward home plate when deciding whether to send an oncoming baserunner home. This gives the coach a little extra time to make the decision to hold or send the runner. By letting the baserunner round third and begin his sprint for home, the coach gains time to watch the play develop (e.g., to see if the ball is fielded cleanly or bobbled in the outfield). Even if the coach and baserunner are a third of the way toward the plate, the coach can still hold the runner at third by using hand and verbal signals to stop him and send him back to third base. During your baserunning drills, you can get your baserunners accustomed to finding the third-base coach as much as a third of the way to home plate. Most umpires will allow this, as it is considered good coaching technique so long as the coach doesn't *interfere* with the play and *immediately returns to his coaching box*. The coach shouldn't touch and *must never* physically aid a baserunner. Also, the coach must always try to get out of the fielders' way and avoid being struck by the ball.

The Mental Aspects of Baserunning

A good player always knows the score, the inning, and the number of outs. It is the game situation that dictates how to run the bases. If you are ahead, or the score is tied, or there is no score early in the game, run the bases with daring. Take chances. If you are behind, play more cautiously.

For example, let's say it is the last inning, you are behind 4-0, and your batter leads off the inning with a base hit. There is a 50-50 chance that he can stretch it into a double. Should he go?

We answer an emphatic "No!" You need four runs to tie and five to win. There will have to be a good deal more offense from your team to get those runs, so it doesn't make sense to try for an extra base and risk getting thrown out. Sure, taking that extra base successfully will remove the force-out at second, and eliminate the double-play situation, but getting thrown out stretching a hit when you need so much additional offense is a bad gamble. Play for one sure base at a time.

On the other hand, if you were *ahead* 4-0 in the same situation, you should be aggressive and daring, keeping the pressure on the defense. Therefore, try for the extra base.

The situation dictates how you run the bases. And good baserunners (and base coaches) are always aware of the situation.

Poorly coached teams always run the bases the same way regardless of the game situation. The score, the inning, the number of outs have no bearing on the team's style of play. This brings to mind automobile drivers, many of whom drive the same way, whatever the road conditions may be. Try to make this analogy to your players: A prudent driver uses extra caution when driving over snow-covered or slippery roads, for example, leaving extra space between himself and any traffic ahead of him. Similarly, a prudent. softball player should run the bases more cautiously when the opponents have a big lead. One extra base or one extra score doesn't mean much when your opponents have plowed you under a blizzard of runs.

Baserunning Drills

Before beginning baserunning drills, all players should warm up and stretch (see Chapter I). We like our players to take a slow lap or two around the park and then form several lines on the right field line behind first base. There, with the first players in each line running simultaneously, they push off an imaginary base set on the foul line and simulate a steal of second base, but run at about half speed. Then they walk back to their respective lines and continue to run imaginary steals, slowly increasing their speed to three-quarter speed and faster, until they are running all-out sprints to second. This running slowly and increasing speed is a good warm-up used in conjunction with stretching.

Running Out Ground Balls

Your players must always sprint out ground balls to the infield, taking off immediately after the ball is hit, not hesitating because they think the ball may be foul. Teach them to run out *all* grounders and let the umpire call it fair or foul (the good umpire points and yells "Foul!" but only points fair). Even a ground ball that is clearly foul but that spins back into fair territory before it passes first or third is a fair ball.

The player should take his initial step toward first with his rear foot. This will make the run to first a half step faster than if he takes the first step with his front foot. (The left-handed hitter would make his first step a crossover step with the left foot while pivoting on the right foot.) The runner should sprint all the way on the balls of his feet, not watching the ball, but keying on first base and listening for instructions from the first-base coach. He should overrun first base by a good margin. Too many youngsters try to defy the laws of motion by hitting first and coming to an immediate stop. This results in their slowing down too early, and may cause them to be out when they should have been safe.

Runners should avoid taking a long final stride or leap when getting to the bag, and should not slide into first (see exception below). A runner should hit first base with whichever foot happens to be there at the time (not stutter-stepping in an attempt to hit the bag with a particular foot) and should look down at the bag while stepping on the front edge of it. (You may want younger players to aim for the middle of the bag).

A common misconception is that if you turn toward second base, you are liable to be tagged out by the first baseman. The truth is that a baserunner may turn either way after overrunning first; in order to be liable (umpires call this being "in jeopardy"), the umpire must rule that you made an attempt to advance to second. (This play is described in Appendix F). Some coaches like their baserunners to turn toward second after overrunning first base because they may be in a better position to advance to second if the ball is misplayed. In any case, the runner should (a) avoid making any motion that might appear to the umpire as an attempt to advance, and (b) locate the ball after tagging first.

Teach your baserunners to run to first in foul territory, especially if a throw is being made by a fielder near home plate. There is a line (real or imaginary) in foul territory running parallel to and 3 feet from the foul line, which covers the last half of the distance to first. This is considered a haven for baserunners, and as long as a runner is in this area he will not be called out if hit by a throw. If he is hit when he is not within this area he may be ruled out for interference.

Again, baserunners should run on the balls of the feet, leaning forward with the body weight, pumping their arms vigorously straight forward and back (not across the body). After stepping on the bag, the runner should turn his head to the right, which protects his face, and may help him locate a ball that has gotten away from the first baseman. We like our runners to key on the first baseman while running out an infield hit, to tell them whether or not they should slide. If an infielder's throw draws him off the bag toward home plate, the runner should slide. Sliding makes it harder for the first baseman to make a successful sweep tag (first sackers are taught, in this situation to swing the glove around quickly to try to tag the runner before he touches first). With luck, as the first baseman sweeps the tag toward the runner, it will pass over his head as the runner "hits the dirt." To teach this baserunning technique, have your players sprint to first, keying on the first baseman, and occasionally have the first sacker come off the bag toward the home-plate side. If he comes off, the runner slides, if not, the runner goes in standing up, and overruns first. Coaches call this "reading" the first baseman. Remember, players who run with enthusiasm and hustle end up well down the right-field line when overrunning first.

A good way to drill on running out infield grounders is to have a single line of players at home plate. Have the first player take a swing (without a bat) at an imaginary ball, then sprint to first. When he is about halfway to first, the second player takes his pretend swing and sprints to first, and play continues until everyone gets a turn. Baserunners return to home plate after each turn and await the next repetition. As players run through the bag, coaches can correct such errors as slowing down too early or missing the base because of not looking down at the bag.

A variation on this drill is to use two lines, the second one running from third base to second base, but pretending to be running from home to first. The two-line method saves time, giving everyone more repetitions, while the first method gives players more time to catch their breath between repetitions. The two-line format also allows for a type of relay race. Put an equal number of players in each line, and have a coach for each line who yells, "Go!" when a player's foot touches the bag. This is the signal for the next runner to take off. For this relay race you can eliminate the pretend swing, and, if the lines are not even, make a player from the short-handed line run twice.

Running Out Fly Balls

Get your runners sprinting as fast and as far as they can on all fly balls. A speedy runner can make it to second base when a high infield or outfield pop-up is misplayed. Get a line of runners at home and a set of fielders in the field. Hit high pops and fly balls to different positions and get the players used to sprinting them out even if they look like routiners.

Base Hit to the Outfield

If a player hits the ball to the outfield, he should execute what we call the "question-mark" turn. As he gets about 15 to 20 feet from first, he dips or loops out about 3 to 5 feet into foul territory. This turn resembles the shape of a question mark and keeps speeding runners from shaking hands with the right fielder as their momentum tends to drive them in his direction. On this turn, try to get runners to hit the inside of the bag with the left foot and lean in toward the pitcher's plate. It is important not to slow down to hit first base, even if it means hitting the bag with the right foot. They should drive the left arm and shoulder down and attempt to get in a straight line with second as soon as possible. The extra steps into foul territory on the

FIGURE 6-1　　　　　　　　**FIGURE 6-2**

QUESTION MARK TURN: *As the runner gets about 15 to 20 feet from first, she dips out about 3 to 5 feet into foul territory. She tries to hit the inside of the bag with her left foot and then leans in toward the pitcher's plate, getting into a straight line with second as quickly as possible.*

way to first are a technique to help the player get in a straight line with second more quickly, saving steps in the long run.

Many players are reluctant to take too many steps into foul territory, and tend to take only a step or two, fearing that to take more would waste time. Train them to veer just outside (to the right of) the 3 foot line, but not more than a foot or two outside. Use a stop watch to time your players making the turn, first without veering foul, and then using the question-mark turn. Show them the logic of taking extra steps early to save even more steps later.

To teach this technique, place a cone in foul territory at the spot where you want the runners to veer out, and instruct them to run outside of this marker. Place a second marker at first base about 10 feet toward second, and tell them to try to get *inside* that one. Your players should use the same question-mark technique when running from first to third and from second to home.

Get your players thinking one base ahead. In other words, as a player takes his question-mark turn and rounds first, he should be thinking about taking second. He should round the base at top speed and go at least a third of the distance to second if the ball is hit to left field, slightly less if hit to center or right. If the outfielder is foolish enough to throw behind the baserunner, the runner should sprint to the next base when the ball leaves the outfielder's hand (watch out for fake throws). He should keep his eyes on the ball as the outfielder plays it. A bobble in the outfield may allow him to take second, but only if he takes that big turn at first, and does so without slowing down.

If the runner holds at first, he should continue to watch the ball, and not turn his back to the play, as the throw may get away from its intended receiver. Runners must take care not to get picked off, as some teams have their outfielders get the ball right in to second base, and whoever takes the throw immediately fires to first.

If the hit was to left field or left centerfield, the runner should round first, come to a stop a third of the way to second, and then push off the right foot, turning in toward the diamond (left shoulder in), to return to first. If the ball was hit to right field or right center, he should push off his left foot after stopping, turning his right shoulder in toward the diamond, and return to first while watching the outfielder and his throw.

When youth players reach a base, they tend to think their job is done. We must teach them *always to think about advancing to the next base*. For example, when a runner stops at third base, he should immediately look home. Sometimes the catcher leaves home plate unguarded and goes to fetch his mask without calling a time out. The runner may be able to score a run that is a great spirit-lifter for his team, and an equally great spirit-demoralizer for the opponents. Teach your players never to be satisfied with the base they have reached, but to think ahead to the next base—and when they get there, think ahead to the next one.

First-Base Coach Instructions Drill

This drill gets your players in the habit of responding to your first-base coach's instructions. Players line up at home plate. Each takes a dry swing, sprints to first, and reacts to the coach's verbal and visual signals. The coach might yell out, "Run hard, dig! dig! dig! right through the bag!" or "Take a big turn!" or "Go to second, two! two! two!" The coach should rotate his left arm in large clockwise circles to indicate "Take second!"

We also use a command called "Up to you!" when coaching first or third base. For balls hit out in front of the runner, where he has a clear view of the play, we like to let an experienced runner decide on his own if he should go or hold. He knows his speed and abilities better than anyone else, so we are apt to give him the "up to you" signal if the play looks close. For example, we may hold a runner at third telling him that the ball is coming in to the catcher. Then, if the ball gets away from the catcher, and the runner starts off the bag, we might call out, "Up to you, up to you!" This is part of what we have called "reading" the play. The baserunner must observe the actions of the fielders and the position of the ball, and react accordingly.

Running from First Base

There is no real leading off base in softball. In fast-pitch games, the baserunner may leave his base when the pitcher releases the pitch. In slow-pitch softball, the runner must wait until the ball reaches the plate, which, for all practical purposes, means when the ball is hit. There is no pick-off from the pitcher in fast- or slow-pitch

SQUARE UP TO INFIELD: The runner faces second, placing her right foot on the edge of the bag and her left foot a stride ahead of the base. She pushes off with the right foot when the pitch is released (when the pitch reaches the plate in slow pitch), takes several steps, squares up to the infield and reads the hit.

FIGURE 6-3   **FIGURE 6-4**

softball, but once a pitch is released, there is the possibility of a pick-off from the catcher in fast-pitch games.

In fast-pitch, the runner should face second, placing his right foot on the edge of the bag and his left foot a stride in front of the base. He should push off his right foot when the pitch is released, take several steps, square up to the infield and watch the ball, reading the hit. From this squared-up position, the runner will pivot on his right foot and crossover with his left foot to advance on a hit. The same "leading" technique should be used in slow-pitch except that the runner pushes off first base only after the ball reaches the plate.

Also, in fast-pitch, any time the pitcher holds the ball in the 16-foot-diameter pitching circle, all runners must return to the base they held or advance to the next base, or they will be called out. So, in fast-pitch games, a baserunner should look for signals in between pitches while he is on the base, and leave the base when the pitch is released. If the ball is not hit and it comes back to the pitcher in his circle, the runner must immediately go back to his base or advance to the next one.

The Rolling Start

If the bases are not stationary, you may want your runners to push off the ground while keeping contact with the side of the base. Many players lean back with the pitcher's motion and time their break from the bag with the release of the pitch. This technique, sometimes called a "rolling start," gets the runner's momentum moving toward the next base. It should only be used with experienced players.

To execute this maneuver, a player should stand with his left foot on the edge of the bag closest to the next base and his right foot behind the bag (on the side of the base away from the infield). The toe of the front foot is on the ground and the heel is on the bag for a better push-off. The runner times his move, taking off with the back foot slightly before the ball is released—when the pitcher's pivot foot clears the pitcher's plate. This occurs a fraction of a second before the ball leaves the pitcher's hand. Again, the runner should face second but turn his head toward the pitcher. (In slow-pitch, he would follow the ball all the way to the plate before taking off). Sometimes, umpires will mistakenly think your baserunner is leaving his base early because they see motion on the part of the runner before the pitch is released. It is a good idea to alert the officials *before the game* to the fact that you will be employing this baserunning technique. They will be more likely to see the play correctly if they are not surprised by it.

During a bunt attempt (fast-pitch), the runner should take his "lead" after the pitch is released, but hold up until he is sure that the

FIGURE 6-5   **FIGURE 6-6**

ROLLING START: *Proper technique allows the runner to get momentum moving toward the next base.*

ball is bunted on the ground. A popped up bunt can lead to an easy double play if the runner at first is careless, and a missed bunt attempt could make him susceptible to a pick-off by the catcher. Also, we see too many baserunners doubled up after line shots are fielded in the infield. In both fast- and slow-pitch, and at any base, a runner must learn to "freeze on a line drive" unless there are two outs. He must hold his position (freeze) until he is sure that the liner is through the infield for a hit.

We want our baserunners to break up possible double plays by sliding hard and clean into second base. The spikes should be down, not up in the fielder's face, chest or waist area. Our intent is to break up the double play by preventing the pivot man's throw to first. If we cannot prevent it, we hope to distract the pivot man and/or force him to make a bad throw to first. We never aim to injure the pivot man.

Sometimes when a fly ball is hit to the outfield with a runner on first, the runner goes half way to second, anticipating a routine catch, and the ball is misplayed and not caught. As the runner takes off for second, the outfielder recovers the ball and throws to second to retire him. Youth players seem to have two problems with this play. One is that they have trouble understanding that this is a force out. The other is that their idea of halfway is different from the coaches' idea of halfway. They seem to think that halfway means several steps off the bag. Many of those who do go halfway tend to start back towards first before the ball is caught (or dropped), as they anticipate an easy catch. They are thinking about retreating instead of thinking *one base ahead*.

We teach our players on first *never to let the second baseman tag them out on a ground ball*. They should make the second baseman throw the ball to the shortstop covering second to "buy time" for the batter-baserunner to reach first. The baserunner on first should stop, and even retreat towards first if necessary, to avoid being tagged out. Even if there are two outs, make the fielder throw the ball. The more people that handle a ball, the more chances for an error.

Runners at First—Reaction Drill

A good drill for youngsters to work on their baserunning from first base is to set up three or four lines of players near first base. Have one line at first base, another a few feet closer to home and the third several feet toward right field. The first players in each line do the drill simultaneously and then get at the end of their line. The coach calls out the play (ground ball, or pop-up, or fly ball to left, etc.) and watches the baserunners react.

The Steal of Second

The steal in fast-pitch softball may be the most effective offensive maneuver available to a team. Some youth leagues have so little success in preventing the steal that they outlaw it altogether or use the slow-pitch baserunning rule—runners may leave their base only after the ball reaches the plate. We teach our young base-stealers to turn their head quickly toward home plate when they are about halfway to second. The idea is not to run to second while looking home, but to throw your head briefly in that direction, hoping to pick up some visual clue about the play. Did the ball get away from the catcher? Can the runner advance all the way to the next base? Is a throw in flight? Often the runner catches sight of something that gives him an advantage in completing the steal successsfully or advancing further. Some coaches call this the "peek technique" of base stealing. Experienced players also should use the "rolling start" technique described above when they steal.

FIGURE 6-7
PEEK TECHNIQUE: *The runner, while stealing, throws her head briefly toward home to pick up some visual clue about the play.*

Runner on First—Fly Ball—Less than Two Outs

When there is a fly ball to right field with less than two outs, we want our baserunner to face the right fielder and go halfway to second. If the ball drops, he sprints for second. If it is caught, he sprints back to first. On a fly to center or left field, he can go as much as three-fourths of the way and still safely advance or retreat, depending on whether the ball is caught or not.

Sometimes, with runners at first and third, the runner from first can tag up on a fly because the defense is more concerned about throwing home to get the lead runner. This is true for a short or medium fly, but on a deeper drive they will probably throw to second, conceding the run. Be careful about tagging up from first on fly balls, as a speedy batter might pass the tagging runner. If this happens, the batter is out even if the ball is not caught. It is the first-base coach's job to inform the batter of the potential problem as he nears first base. It is always a good idea to tag up on fly balls that are obviously foul.

Going from First to Third on a Single

Generally, the baserunner from first should try to take third on a hit to right field. The defense needs a good throw, a successful catch of the throw, and an effective tag of a sliding runner to make the out. The odds are in the offense's favor. We teach our runners to pick up the third-base coach when they are about halfway to second base. The coach will be waving the runner on to third or holding him at second. If he waves the runner on, he will give further instructions about whether to slide, stand up, or continue home. If the hit is to left- or center-field, out in front of the runner, he should use his own judgment about whether to advance. Coaches may use the "up to you" instruction discussed previously.

A good drill is to set up a line of runners at first, with the outfielders, third baseman, shortstop, second baseman and third-base coach in their customary positions. Have a coach fungo base hits to all the outfielders who then try to throw the runner out at third. The runner picks up the coach on balls hit to right and uses his own judgment on balls hit in front of him. He shouldn't slow down when reading the coach. The infielders play their normal positions, lining up outfielders' throws, taking cut-offs, etc. After advancing to third, each runner jogs back to first and gets at the end of the line.

Two-Base Hit Drill

Line up your players at home. On your command, the first player takes a dry swing and runs out a double. He takes his question mark turn, hits first base with his left foot, leans in, gets in a straight line with second as quickly as possible, and goes into second base standing up. Then he jogs to third and home and gets at the end of the line there. Each subsequent player takes his dry swing and starts for first when the previous runner is halfway to first base.

Running from Second Base

The runner at second should advance on a ground ball hit to the right side (first or second baseman) when there is no one else on base. He should hold on a grounder to the left side (third baseman or shortstop) or back to the pitcher. Some coaches teach their players to go on a grounder to the shortstop's left or on one hit right at him but hit slowly. These would be tough plays for the shortstop who would probably concede third base to the runner and try to retire the batter. Similarly, a runner can advance on a grounder to third when the third baseman has to charge the ball. With younger players, we recommend keeping it simple. If the ball is hit to the right side they should advance to third. If not, they should stay at second. We see too many players try to advance on ground balls back to the pitcher or routiners right at the shortstop. They either get thrown out immediately, or get put out after a run-down. Often a runner at second will try to advance on a ground ball to the shortstop's right. Let's say there is one out. The shortstop gloves the ball and throws to the third baseman who makes the tag. The runner is out and the batter is safe at first with two outs. If the runner at second had held, the shortstop would have been forced to make the long throw to first. The shortstop's throw may have been wild, or the runner may have beaten the throw, making it first and second with one out. As another option, the runner may have taken off after the shortstop's long throw to first.

In fast pitch games the runner at second must be alert for passed balls and wild pitches as well as pick-off attempts from the catcher. If the catcher throws to first for a pick-off, an alert runner can advance to third base, but watch out for fake throws.

Runner on Second—Fly Ball—Less than Two Outs

With less than two outs, the runner on second should tag up on flies to right, right-center, center, and deep left-center. He must then decide whether to advance after the catch or to "draw a throw" by bluffing. To aid in this decision, he and the third-base coach must consider factors such as the strength and accuracy of the fielder's throwing arm, wind direction and velocity, and the baserunner's speed. If the fly is hit to left, the runner should go about 1/3 of the way to third base, face the left fielder, and be ready to go either way depending on whether the ball is caught.

Scoring From Second on a Hit

Baserunners must get used to reading the third-base coach when advancing from second on a hit, both before and after rounding third. As the runner approaches third the coach may be in the coach's box signalling the runner to score. The coach may then move down the line toward home and continue signalling the runner home, or he may stop him and quickly send him back to third.

A good drill involves lining up all players at second base and having the third base coach in his box yell out "Go!" On the "Go" command, the first player takes off for third, reading the coach who may stop him at third standing up or sliding. The coach may also wave the runner all the way home or move down the line and then hold him, sending him back to third repeating the command "Dive!

Dive! Dive!" Each runner waits for the "Go" signal before taking off. Players jog back to the end of the line at second when done with their turn.

The Steal of Third

The steal of third is generally not a good percentage move in youth softball. The catcher has a short throw. Sometimes, with two outs and a weak hitter at the plate, it is worth the gamble. The throw to third may go into left field and the offense "steals" a run as the baserunner continues home. A right-handed batter makes it harder for the catcher to get a clear shot at the runner. Coaches have to gauge their opponents' defensive ability. Some defensive units are so weak that the steal is automatic, no matter what the situation is.

Three Base Hit Drill

This drill works the same as the two-base hit drill except that the runner must execute two question-mark turns, one at first and one at second. He goes into third standing up and jogs back to home plate to get at the end of the line there.

"Leading" From Third Base

When the runner comes off the base he should run into foul territory. If he is hit by a batted ball while the ball is foul, it is a foul ball. If, however, he is hit by a batted ball that is fair, the runner is out. In slow-pitch softball the ball is dead (no play can be made) if not hit. But in fast-pitch the catcher may attempt a pick-off, so the runner should return to third in fair territory to make this a tougher play for the catcher. The runner should move quickly back to third, squaring up to the infield and looking back at the catcher as he goes.

Runner on Third—Fly Ball—Less than Two Outs

We like our players to tag from third on almost all fly balls when there are less than two outs (on short flies where there is little chance of tagging and scoring, we may go 1/3 of the way). Tag up even if the hit looks like a sure run. If you go halfway and the outfielder makes a miraculous catch, you may not have time to retouch third and then score. The runner should face home, planting one foot on the bag

FIGURE 6-8

TAG UP FROM THIRD: *The runner faces home and keeps one foot on the bag while waiting for the coach's verbal and/or visual signal to advance.*

and the other a stride forward and pointing directly home. He should wait for the coach's verbal and/or visual signal to go. The coach should move down the line toward home and try to position himself so that he can see the catch, and the runner can see him. He should raise one arm like the starter in a footrace and drop the arm, simultaneously yelling "Go!" when the ball is first touched by the fielder. On all fly balls, a tagging runner may legally advance as soon as the ball is touched by a fielder.

We find that many youth players will leave early (before the ball is first touched) if you let them watch the catch and decide on their own when to take off. Therefore, we practice the technique described above with one coach hitting fly balls to the outfield and our baserunners at third looking home and waiting for the third-base coach's signal to advance.

Runner at Third—Ground Ball

With runners at first and third, less than two outs, and a ground ball, we like to send the runner from third home because the infielders are likely to go for the double play. Of course, the third-base coach must consider other factors, such as whether the infield is playing in, who will be coming to bat next, the score, the inning, etc.

With no one else on base and less than two outs the runner at third may want to wait for the infielder's throw to first before taking off for home. With runners at second and third, the runner at third must read the ground ball and react quickly, breaking for home or holding his ground.

Inside the Park Homerun Drill

This is similar to the two- and three-base hit drills except that three question mark turns are required. Players line up at home, take a dry swing, and sprint out an "inside the parker." Make sure that there are no collisions at home plate by having your players who are taking dry swings give the runner coming home the "right of way." Stationary bases (Hollywood-type, tie down, or breakaway bases) are best for practicing baserunning. Throw down bags tend to slip out from underfoot.

Miscellaneous Baserunning Tips

Once your players master the technique for these drills, get the defense in position and hit balls so that your runners can react to the way balls are hit and how the defense plays. Game-like conditions help them learn to read the hit and react accordingly. Working on baserunning during batting practice is an effective use of time (see Chapter IX).

Make sure your players tag up on fly balls that are obviously foul. This is especially important if the fielder's back is to the infield and his momentum is carrying him away from the diamond. Often, by the time the fielder makes a running catch of a foul and realizes that a runner has tagged, it is too late to get the runner.

Sliding into first on close plays won't get runners there any quicker (it actually slows them down), but it makes a pretty good "smoke screen" and many umpires (even experienced ones) will call the runner safe.

Teach your players to stay in a run-down as long as possible. This allows other trailing runners to advance, and the more throws the defense makes the more likely they'll make an error. Runners should also try to bump into a fielder who is in the baseline without possession of the ball. This is obstruction on the fielder's part.

Baserunners can stop or even run backwards to avoid a tag at any base except first. He may *stop* to avoid a tag on his way to first, but is declared out if he runs backwards to avoid or delay being tagged.

Teach your runners never to leave a base unless they are absolutely sure the umpire has declared them out. Sometimes the umpire is unsure of what to call. If the runner abandons the base, he helps the official by, in effect, calling himself out. Similarly, the runner should never step off the base to dust himself off or tie his shoe until a time-out. Time is not out when a player asks for a time-out. It is out when the umpire *recognizes* the request for a time-out.

Teach your base coaches always to tell a runner where the ball is after he slides into a base. He may not realize that it is in the fielder's glove, or that it has rolled away from him, etc.

Sliding

Youth players generally get even less instruction in sliding than they do in baserunning. Many coaches fear their players will get injured during sliding practice. In actuality, the chances are greater that youths will get hurt sliding in games if they *don't* have sliding practice. We like to have our first sliding sessions in a large playground sandbox. This works well, but you have to be careful that there isn't too much soft sand slowing down the slider's forward momentum, or players will learn to go into a slide too late. Some coaches like to practice sliding on wet grass, with players in stocking feet. They hose the grass down slightly and make sure the players wear old clothes suitable for grass stains. Still others prefer sliding on the ballfield in a game-like situation. Whatever the case, sliding pads will help prevent nasty "strawberry" bruises.

Players should walk through a few practice slides at first. Next, they should jog into the slide, then run. Another way to teach beginners to slide is to get them into the "crab" position. This is a four point stance where both feet and hands are on the ground supporting the body with the belly facing up. On the signal from the coach the players can release their hands and feet from under them and go into a simulated slide. The players hold this position until the coach checks each one for proper head, leg and arm position. The coach of younger children may want his players in the crab position to kick out the feet only. After proper leg position is mastered, then the coach can have his players combine the action of releasing the hands with kicking out the feet.

Sliders must learn to keep their hands and arms from contacting the ground—a cause of frequent bone bruises and scraped elbows. Many players go into their slides too late, and jam their lead arm or leg into a stationary base. And players often get injured when they change their mind after beginning a slide. Once a player makes a decision to slide, he must always go through with the slide.

Another way sliders get hurt is by jumping into the slide, performing a crash landing or belly-flop, and coming down hard on the backside or stomach. The slider should glide in, not jump to a base. All of these faults in technique can be corrected with sliding practice, and a well-executed slide is one of the great feelings that softball has to offer.

The slide should start about two body lengths from the base. As the take-off begins, the arms should be thrown up to avoid bone bruises on the palms (some players hold dirt in each hand to keep the hands up, closed and protected). The feet go forward and the upper body goes backwards with the slider landing on his bottom. From this position he can turn his body to one side or another, aiming for the part of the bag where it will be hardest for the fielder to tag him. The take-off should always be low to the ground, and this initial technique for going into a slide is the same for all slides.

The Bent-Leg Slide

The bent leg slide, like all slides, starts about two body lengths from the base. The slider should bend one leg under his body and slide on his buttocks, keeping the top foot about six inches off the ground. This slide can be made with either leg bent and tucked under the other. It is the top foot that touches the base (the heel hits first). When reaching the base, the player can plant the bottom foot on the ground and push off to get back up to standing position. This slide is like sitting down quickly and bouncing back up. A player can do a bent leg slide to either side of the base and execute a hand tag with the hand closer to the base. Keep the top leg up to avoid catching the spikes in the dirt. The slider doesn't have to bounce back up, but this slide is ideal for the maneuver, allowing him to quickly continue to the next base if the opportunity presents itself.

The Hook Slide

The hook slide is used to evade a tag. When the slider lands, both feet are extended toward the base. After contacting the base, the toe and instep of one foot hook the bag as the body momentum carries the slider forward. A common error is to bend the hooking leg too soon, causing the slider to contact the bag later than he should. The outside foot continues past the base (off the ground to prevent catching in the dirt). This is a good slide to use when breaking up a double play, allowing you to lean one way or the other, while the bent-leg slide is a more upright and balanced slide.

FIGURE 6-9
BENT-LEG SLIDE: Proper technique—one leg under the body, sliding on the buttocks, arms up.

HOOK SLIDE: Used to evade a tag.
FIGURE 6-10

The Head-First Slide

The head-first slide is not really dangerous except at home plate. We don't want our runners sliding head first into a burly catcher in full gear. The slider cups his hands to prevent injury to the fingers and dives low. No belly flops! The hands are outstretched fully to reach for the base. This slide is recommended for returning to a base after a line drive is caught and a fielder tries to double the runner up, or during a pick-off attempt from the catcher in fast-pitch softball.

The Fall-Away or Decoy Slide

This slide (also called the flop-over slide) is used when the defensive player has the ball and is waiting to tag the slider. The idea is to slide outside and past the base, so the slide is started late. For example, while sliding into second, the body would be out toward center field. While flat on his back, the slider shows the would-be tagger his left arm and, as he passes the base, he whips the arm away. He rolls over quickly onto his belly and touches or grabs the back corner of the bag with his right hand. This move often tricks the

FIGURE 6-11

HEAD-FIRST SLIDE: *Arms extended fully to reach for the base.*

FIGURE 6-12

DECOY SLIDE: *The slider slides past the bag, shows the fielder his left arm, and rolls over quickly onto his belly and touches the back corner of the bag with the right hand.*

tagger into coming after the runner. It can be done from the opposite side as well. For example, at home plate the runner may slide to the infield side showing the catcher his right hand. He then whips the right hand away, rolls over and tags the back of the plate with his left hand.

Reading the Receiver

Whenever the throw is coming from behind the runner, he should "read" the reactions of the receiver and slide accordingly. If the fielder appears to be shifting to one side of the bag to take the throw, slide on the opposite side to give him the smallest possible target. Sliding away from the tag is sliding strategically. Of course, at third base, watch the coach giving verbal and visual signals, and at home read the on-deck hitter (or runner who just scored) who should be there picking up the hitter's bat and giving the oncoming runner directions. If the coach or on-deck hitter gives no help, slide. When in doubt, always slide.

FIGURE 6-13
FIGURE 6-14

Sliding Drills

Place an even number of players at each base, including home plate. Place a first baseman on first who will pretend to be taking throws from the infield. He should occasionally come off the base to simulate a wide throw pulling him off the bag. On command from the coach, the first player in each line takes off. The runner from home runs through the bag at first, sliding only if the first baseman comes off the bag. The runner from first does a fall-away slide. The runner from second does a bent-leg slide, and the runner from third does a hook slide. Change the slides every so often. If you have the personnel, station one coach at each base to correct technique. After reaching a base, the player gets at the end of the line at that base. Players waiting for their turn must keep out of the oncoming runner's way. Use a third-base coach who can tell the runner from second where to slide, helping him to elude an imaginary tag. For example, if the coach "sees" that a throw will take the third baseman toward home plate, he should get his runner sliding for the left-field side of the bag.

Here is a sliding drill race. Form two lines with an equal number of players, one running from first to second and another running from third to home. If the lines are unequal, one player can take two turns. Place a coach at second and a coach at home. Each player must sprint to the next base and slide (coach indicates head-first, hook or bent-leg). When the slider touches the base, the coach signals the next runner to go. The first line to get all its runners to touch base wins the race.

This is an excellent drill for teaching runners who have just scored to help subsequent runners advancing to the plate. Place half your runners at third and half at second. On the coach's signal, both runners sprint to home. The runner from third scores and picks up the bat (the imaginary batter's), not only to get it out of the way, but to hold it up or down to tell the oncoming runner to stand or slide. The runner from second also scores, reading the previous runner's signal to stand or slide. After the play, the runner from third drops the bat anywhere near home plate and jogs to the end of the line at second. The runner from second jogs to the end of the line at third, and the next two runners take off. Players helping at home plate in games should not only tell the runner whether to slide, but also *where* to slide, as they can see the trajectory of the throw.

VII. Fast-Pitch Pitching

As in baseball, pitching is 70% to 90% of the game in fast-pitch softball. And like baseball hurlers, physical fitness is essential for softball pitchers. A pitcher needs to stretch, run, jump rope, and do other exercises more than any other player, to increase strength, coordination, and endurance. Few coaches will argue that, in any sport, a stronger athlete is a better athlete.

The most important thing a pitcher can do is throw strikes. The sooner you sell your pitchers on this point, the better off your team will be. It is more important to throw strikes than to have a blazing fastball, a great rise, or a devastating drop. If the pitcher throws strikes, the team can win (provided the rest of the team can make the plays behind him). Some college teams play intrasquad games with a machine pitching to both squads. A pitching machine set to throw fastballs at a medium to fast speed delivers 90% strikes and, even though it throws no "junk," the games often end up 3-2, or 4-3. Strikes force the hitters to swing, and give your teammates the opportunity to make fielding plays. If the pitcher throws ball after ball, walks lead to more pressure on the defense, which leads to errors and high-scoring games.

Mental Aspects of Pitching

Pitching requires concentration, control, confidence, and, above all, emotional stability (composure). Pitchers should never show signs of being upset over hits, errors or walks, and they must never get overly excited about strikeouts and putouts. They must concentrate each inning on getting the lead-off hitter. Coaches are fond of saying, "Get the leading lady." To get the lead-off hitter, the pitcher must try to get ahead in the count. His first pitch should be the one he can most consistently throw for a strike. For most pitchers this is the fastball, not a breaking ball or change-up. When the other team gets its lead-off batter on base, their chances of scoring increase dramatically, especially in fast-pitch softball where the offense can steal and bunt. Pitchers often "let up" with two outs and become vulnerable. Teach your pitchers to believe in themselves and to be mentally tough throughout the game.

131

Reading Hitters

Pitchers and catchers must become adept at reading the hitters. By this we mean analyzing batting stance, position in the box, and warm-up swings. A pitcher should look for any information that will help him get the hitter out. Pitch "in on the hands" to a hitter who crowds the plate. Throw to the outside corner if a hitter stands away from the plate. Batters with wide stances generally have trouble with high inside fastballs. Those with a long stride have trouble with off-speed pitches. Throw a change-up to a batter who just pulled a drive foul.

Pitching Strategy

One of the most effective things a pitcher can do is vary the speed of his pitches. Hitting is timing for the most part. Pitching, then, should be concerned with disrupting the hitter's timing. A pitcher should stick with his best pitch, the one he can throw for a strike, most of the time. Sometimes it is a good idea to throw a change-up when the hitter is ahead in the count and probably looking for a fastball. Changing speeds and locations is the key to disrupting the hitter's timing. Wasting an occasional pitch is often good strategy. If two fastballs go for strikes, make the next pitch a breaking ball, low and away, to set up the hitter for a fastball on the following pitch. In a sacrifice bunt situation, try to throw strikes which are high in the strike zone. These are difficult to bunt, are often popped up for an easy out, and, with bad baserunning, may even result in a double play.

Developing the Youth Pitcher

Fast-pitch softball pitchers are developed, not born. By working hard at the techniques and fundamentals of pitching, a youngster can become an effective softball pitcher. But the process involves practicing long hours. Many successful adult pitchers tell the same story—as youngsters they put in many hours throwing alone against a wall or pitching to a patient friend. Most pitchers grip the ball across the seams, but holding it with the seams works just as well for some players. Most beginning pitchers use three fingers, switching to a two-finger grip later if their hands grow large enough. Some youth leagues use a smaller softball (with an 11-inch as opposed to 12-inch circumference) to make it easier for pitchers and fielders to throw the ball accurately. The ball should rest comfortably on the fingers, not back in the palm of the hand. When the ball is held too far back, it is harder to get wrist snap. To get a feel for the release, beginners should grip the ball properly and toss it into the air, letting it roll off their fingertips, from the little finger toward the index finger. This action imparts a left to right spin (for a right-handed pitcher). Next, pitchers should use their wrists to flip the ball higher, concentrating on the wrist snap at the release point.

The Windmill Delivery

The legal delivery in fast-pitch softball is called the windmill. In A.S.A. fast-pitch softball, the pitcher must have his pivot foot on the pitching plate and his non-pivot foot on or behind the plate. The pitcher makes a full revolution of the arm and strides toward the batter with the non-pivot foot, while pushing off the rubber with the pivot foot. The striding foot must land within the 24-inch width of the pitcher's plate.

Using the following three-phase drill, pitchers can perfect a windmill delivery that results in consistent strikes. These procedures involve throwing a ball against a wall in progressively more realistic pitching conditions. They work best if you paint a simulated strike zone on the wall as a target for the pitcher. Also, you may want to use some sort of pitching rubber.

The pitcher should never progress to a new phase until the previous one is mastered.

Phase I. The Release: Start 15 to 20 feet away from the wall. The feet should be shoulder-width apart with the non-pivot foot (left foot for right-handed pitchers) one walking-stride ahead of the right. Both feet remain stationary and flat-footed during this drill, with a little bend in both knees. (We are eliminating the legs in this drill to concentrate on the delivery and the release.) The ball and pitching arm should drop back and up to an overhead position. Hold this position briefly. The wrist should be cocked and there should be a bend in the elbow. Start the pitching motion by pulling the ball down hard and releasing it at the thigh with a strong wrist snap and follow-through. Try to hit the wall about waist-high. The ball is at the 12 o'clock position when overhead, and is released at the 6 o'clock position. During the delivery, keep the little finger and the elbow as close to the body as possible. Field the ball and get ready for the next pitch.

When the pitcher can hit the wall waist high consistently, he should back up. If he rarely hits the target, move him up. Eventually he should get to the regulation pitching distance, which is anywhere from 35 to 46 feet, depending on the age and sex of the pitcher. It is

FIGURE 7-1

FIGURE 7-2

FIGURE 7-3

PHASE I SEQUENCE: *Knees are bent and both feet remain stationary and flat-footed during the drill. The ball and pitching arm should drop back and up to an overhead position. With wrist cocked and a bend in the elbow, hold this position briefly. Next, pull the ball down hard, release it at the thigh with a strong wrist snap, and follow through.*

IGURE 7-4 **FIGURE 7-5** **FIGURE 7-6**

PHASE II SEQUENCE: *The ball and glove are held in front of the pitcher's waist. She begins to bring the ball and glove overhead, keeping them an arm's length away from the body as she does so. As the arms reach the chest area, the pitcher begins taking the ball out of the glove. As the pitching hand reaches the twelve o'clock position, she is back to Phase I, and continues through with the release of the ball.*

FIGURE 7-7 **FIGURE 7-8**

important to note that releasing the ball early results in a low pitch, while releasing late causes a high one. The pitcher should watch where the ball hits the wall, and make any necessary adjustments. Remember, in this drill the feet don't move at all, the body stays square to the plate, and the pitching hand follows through in the direction of the released pitch.

Phase II. The Upswing: In this phase, the pitcher holds the ball and glove in front of him at his waist, in the pitching position. His feet are stationary and in the same position as in Phase I. The ball is in his pitching hand, and both ball and hand are in the glove. He should bring the ball and glove up overhead, keeping them away from the body at arm's length as he does so. As the arms reach 3 o'clock (straight out in front of the chest area), the pitcher begins taking the ball out of his glove. As the ball comes toward the 12 o'clock position, an important shift in the pitching hand occurs. The wrist must rotate the ball so that the thumb changes position from the inside (nearest the body) to the outside (away from the body). This wrist and arm movement bends the elbow, cocks the wrist, and brings the pitcher to the exact same position as in Phase I. Now he brings his arm down and releases the ball at the 6 o'clock position with a strong wrist snap and follow-through. He should stay flat-footed, square to the plate, and not come up on his toes as the ball is released.

Phase III. The Follow-through: The follow-through helps the pitcher's control and speed, and prepares him to become an infielder. The pitcher takes the same initial position as in the other phases, but lengthens the stride a little. The pitch is delivered as in Phase II except that, as the ball is released, the trail leg comes forward a step. The lead leg is still planted, but the trail leg comes forward and lands slightly ahead of it.

When the beginning pitcher has mastered all three phases of this drill, he can begin throwing from the rubber, combining his footwork with the delivery. He should be most concerned with developing control. Next, he should be concerned with building velocity, and a change-up to offset it. Finally, he may want to start adding other pitches to his repertoire.

(Note: Some pitchers like to begin their delivery by dropping the hands down and back before starting the windmill motion. This means that the ball will be released on the second forward swing of the pitching arm past the hip, and may appear to be two revolutions of the arm. Making two revolutions is illegal, but this delivery is actually one revolution, and is permitted. Some pitchers feel they build more momentum with this delivery, called the double-pump, and con-

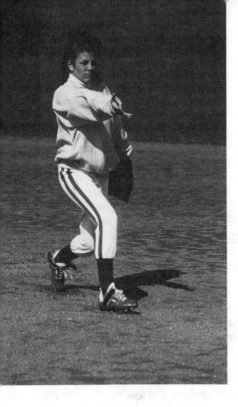

FIGURE 7-9
PHASE III: *The trail foot comes forward during the follow-through.*

sequently throw harder. However, we feel that there is a corresponding loss of control with this style, and recommend that youth pitchers stay with the single-pump delivery.)

Putting it All Together—Mechanics of Fast-pitch Pitching

The pitcher should take a comfortable stance with his feet about shoulder-width apart. The front of the right foot should be hooked over the front of the pitching rubber. The toe of the left foot is touching the back part of the rubber or is just behind the rubber. Many pitchers start their delivery with a slight backward lean, then shift the weight forward to begin the actual pitching motion. The pitcher bends forward at the waist as the pitching arm is brought up. He strides with the left foot simultaneously with the release of the ball. The stride foot must land within the 24-inch width of the pitcher's plate, pointing straight toward home plate. He should push hard off the pitching rubber and snap the wrist as the ball is released. The pivot foot comes up for the follow-through, landing slightly in advance of the striding foot. The feet finish approximately shoulder-width apart and square to home plate. The glove is held up at about chest height in a good defensive position.

Developing Control

The pitcher should work on spot pitching (throwing to specific spots) to develop control. He should practice throwing at the catcher's left shoulder, right shoulder, left knee, right knee, glove, chest, etc. The coach should record the number of hits and misses, and chart results over a period of time. Use a catcher in full gear for this drill, and you may also want a right- or left-handed batter with a batting helmet standing in the batter's box (but not swinging) to make things more realistic. The pitching hand should follow through where the pitcher wants the ball to go.

Many pitchers make an adjustment as the ball is released to hit the corners more accurately. For high, inside pitches (to the righty batter) the ball is gripped and released as discussed earlier, but for high, outside pitches, the pitching hand must rotate 90 degrees (counter clockwise) so that the thumb moves toward the front of the ball on release. In both cases, the ball comes off the fingertips with the same spin which is caused by the ball rolling from the little finger toward the index finger.

For low, outside pitches, turn the ball 90 degrees again and snap the wrist (not the entire arm) across the body. For low, inside pitches, snap the ball straight ahead without turning it 90 degrees, and let it come off the middle fingers instead of spinning it from little finger to index finger. As you might expect, all of this takes a good deal of practice to master.

The Basic Repertoire of Pitches

Remember, the youth pitcher should work on control and changing speeds rather than developing a large repertoire of pitches. Also, since the grip is different for various pitches, the pitcher should take care to hide his pitching hand and ball inside the glove so as not to tip off the hitter.

The Fastball

For a fastball, the pitcher should grip the ball with three fingers spread comfortably apart across the seams. He should step directly toward home plate, snapping his wrist and letting the ball roll off his fingertips, as described above. A pitcher must be able to consistently throw his fastball for a strike.

The Change-up

A softball pitcher needs an off-speed pitch. In fact, he can get by with only two pitches: a fastball and a change-up. Remember, hitting

FIGURE 7-10

THUMB ROTATES 90 DEGREES

FIGURE 7-11

is timing, and good pitching disrupts the hitter's timing. A good way for a pitcher to throw a change-up is to make the motion as close to that of his fastball as possible, but with the ball held back in the palm of the hand. He can throw the ball as hard as his fastball, but will not get the same velocity with this grip and very little, if any, wrist snap. Some pitchers like to use a knuckleball as a change-up (see below). Always keep this pitch low. High change-ups have a tendency of finding their way over the outfield fence. "Low and Slow" is the motto of a smart pitcher with an effective change-up.

The Drop

The grip for the drop is the same as that for the fastball. Most pitchers try to take the thumb off the ball just before the release and snap their wrist over the ball. The fingers roll over the top of the softball, imparting a right to left, downward spin.

The Rise

The rise is held across the seams with the index and middle fingers together. Some pitchers like to tuck the index finger up on a

RISE GRIPS

FIGURE 7-12   **FIGURE 7-13**

seam like a one finger knuckler. The pitcher must bring his hand under the ball at the point of release and snap his wrist, arm, and forearm upward to impart a rapid spin to the ball. The ball must roll over the inside of the middle finger and the first joint of the index finger.

The Knuckleball

The knuckleball is gripped like a fastball except with the middle three fingers tucked under (some pitchers dig the fingertips right into the ball). The thumb and little finger come off the ball during the release, and the ball is pushed out of the hand by the three knuckles without wrist snap. This release imparts no spin to the ball, helping it to "float," and allowing wind currents to move it up or down erratically.

Signals

The trick to giving good signals is to make them simple enough for the pitcher to understand, yet difficult for baserunners and coaches to steal. Let's say 1 is the signal for a fastball, 2 is a change-up and 3 is a rise. The catcher touches his mask, chest protector, and shin

FIGURE 7-14
KNUCKLEBALL GRIP

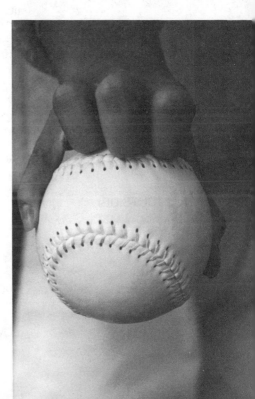

guards, then gives three signals with his fingers. If the mask is touched first, then the first sign is live (1-2-3 is a fastball). If the chest protector is touched first, then the second sign is live (1-3-1 is a rise). Finally, if a shin guard is touched first, the third signal is live (3-2-1 is a fastball).

Keeping Stats

Charting pitches is an analytical tool for use both during and after the game. Coaches can review charts between innings with the pitcher and make adjustments, or they can analyze them after games. In either case, they should look for patterns. Does a particular batter usually hit the first pitch? Does the pitcher consistently miss with his breaking ball? Prepare a sheet with approximately twenty strike zone diagrams (see sample) on it; make enough copies to cover at least thirty-six at-bats versus the pitcher. You can mark the type and location of pitches on these to produce a concise record of your pitcher's deliveries.

Enter the batter's uniform number at the top left and circle the R or the L to indicate right-handed or left-handed hitter. The top line on the

```
            #      (HIGH)        R L


                 ------------------------------------
                        (armpit)
   (OUTSIDE)     :                          :  (INSIDE)

                 :                          :

                 :                          :

                 :                          :
                        (belt)
                 ------------------------------------


   (OUTSIDE)     :                          :  (INSIDE)

                 :                          :

                 :                          :

                 :                          :
                        (knee)
                 ------------------------------------

                        (LOW)
```

strike zone represents the top of the fast-pitch strike zone, the batter's arm pits. A pitch higher than that line would be above the strike zone. The second line down represents the batter's belt area and the third line represents the bottom of the fast-pitch strike zone, the top of the batter's knees. A pitch below the bottom line would be under the strike zone. The lines to the left and right represent the outside and inside corners of the strike zone. (For a left-handed batter the positions for inside and outside would be reversed.)

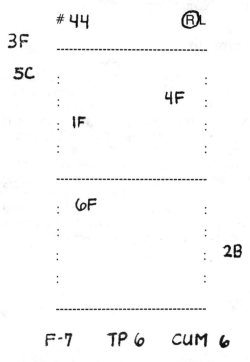

As play progresses, the coach or a designated player marks F for fastball, B for breaking ball, or C for change-up, in the spot on the chart that indicates where the pitch was in relation to the strike zone. The letter is preceded by the number of the pitch (first, second, third, etc.) to the batter. For example, 1F marked in the middle of the lower box would indicate that the first pitch to the hitter was a fastball in the middle of the strike zone and below the belt.

The marked example shows that number 44, a right-handed batter, was thrown a fastball for a strike on the first pitch. The second, pitch, a breaking ball, was inside, and the next offering was a high, outside fastball. Pitch 4 was a fastball for a strike, pitch 5 a change-up for a ball, and the sixth delivery, a fastball, was hit to left-field for a fly out (see notation F-7 in bottom left corner—Appendix F contains information on how to score a game). TP 6 indicates that 6 total pitches were thrown to this batter and CUM 6 tells us that the cumulative pitch count is also 6 (this is the first batter in the game). Charts like this can tell us the percentage of each type of pitch thrown, as well as the percentage of strikes to balls, fastballs to breaking balls, and first pitches thrown for strikes. They not only help us develop our pitchers, but also are effective in helping us decide how to pitch to opposing hitters.

Pregame Warm-Up

Pitchers should do some light running and stretch and warm up their muscles with the rest of the team. It is important to stretch the leg muscles, as leg thrust helps generate velocity. All of this should occur shortly before game time. A pitcher needs to time his warm-up so that he can get completely loose without finishing so early that he begins to tighten up again. He shouldn't have too much time cooling off before stepping onto the pitcher's plate to throw his first pitch. During his warm-up, he should work on all the pitches he will use in the game. When finished, he should wear a windbreaker to conserve the heat generated from the warm-up. During the game, if your team has a long time at bat, instruct your pitcher to throw some additional warm-up pitches, or do some light stretching.

VIII. Slow-Pitch Pitching

Slow-pitch softball is a hitter's game. Everybody's mindset, including the pitcher's, must be that slow-pitch softball means hitting. Your pitcher is not going to dominate the game as he might in fast-pitch. However, there is still a good deal of pitching strategy involved. Since he can't blow the ball by the hitters, the slow-pitch pitcher has to be crafty. He must strive to give up no walks while realizing that he will seldom get a strikeout. He must hit his spots to make the batters contact the ball less solidly, so that his fielders can make the plays.

The legal A.S.A. slow-pitch delivery must reach a height of between 6 and 12 feet from the ground. If the pitch is less than six or more than 12 feet from the ground, the umpire will call an illegal pitch, which is an automatic ball on the batter. However, if the batter swings at the illegal pitch, it becomes legal—a swing and a miss is a strike, a hit out of the park is a homerun. The plate umpire will generally call the illegal pitch, loud enough for the batter and catcher to hear, as soon as it becomes illegal. Since the delivery is slow, the hitter generally has enough time to decide if he wants to swing.

The 6-foot minimum exists to prevent fastballs and ensure plenty of hitting. Some leagues allow an unlimited height to the arc, which gives the pitcher a tremendous advantage. While it is tougher to throw strikes with a very high arc (15 to 20 feet or higher), it is much more difficult to hit those strikes solidly.

To a degree, slow-pitch pitchers can throw the hitter's timing off by varying the arc. The higher the arc, the longer it takes the ball to reach the plate. Conversely, the lower the arc, the quicker the ball reaches the batter. There are still likely to be few strikeouts, but the effect on the hitter's timing may result in less accurate contact, producing pop-ups and fly balls instead of line drives. The idea, then, is to try not to throw two pitches in a row with the same arc, especially not in the same location. Mix it up. Throw one short and outside, then one deep and inside. The hitter may miss the center or top half of the ball, the target they are trained to aim for.

As in fast-pitch softball, the pitchers should analyze a batter's potential weakness and attempt to exploit it. You may want to have your pitcher watch the opponents' batting practice. Examine stances and swings. Find out which hitters, if any, hit the ball well to the opposite field. If the defense leaves right field unattended every time

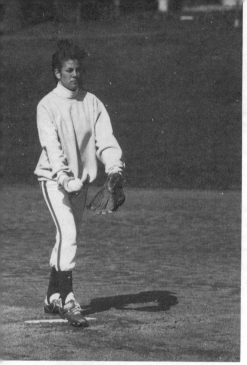 

FIGURE 8-1   **FIGURE 8-2**

SLOW PITCH DELIVERY: *The pitcher drops the pitching hand down and back before the release. One or both feet must be in contact with the*

a right-handed hitter comes to bat, this tells you something about the opposition. If the batting practice is well organized, moving quickly from one batter to the next, this also tells you something about the opposition. Some coaches keep a hitting-tendency chart (tracking where each hitter tends to hit the ball during games), and position their fielders accordingly.

During games, the pitcher can help position players in the field, so, in batting practice, he should look to see who are the long-ball hitters, the singles hitters, the spray hitters and the dead-pull hitters. If the coach instructs his pitcher to move defensive players around, he must inform the fielders that he has given this authority to the pitcher, and fielders must move when directed to do so.

It is the pitcher's job to know which hitters in the line-up he will be facing in each inning. Each inning, after retiring the side, he should go right to the scorekeeper and review who will be coming up in the following inning, and what they did in their previous at-bats. Remember that the 1-2 hitters are usually fast runners with a high on-base percentage. Often, they are good at drawing walks. The 3-4-5 spots are usually the power hitters. These are generally the free swingers. The 6-7-8-9-10-11 hitters are the weaker batters (in the manager's opinion) in descending order of ability. They hit less consistently, and with less power.

FIGURE 8-3

FIGURE 8-4

pitcher's plate. The pitch must reach a height of six to twelve feet from the ground.

FIGURE 8-5

FIGURE 8-6

Mechanics of the Slow-pitch Delivery

The slow-pitch delivery may be the windmill-type, with a 360-degree arc, but this is rarely seen. More often the pitcher makes a full or partial backswing or just holds the ball out in front of his body, then drops the hand down and back six to eight inches before the release. The ball is generally delivered with the palm up, but may be thrown legally palm down. One or both feet must be in contact with the pitcher's plate. The pitch must be delivered on the first forward swing of the pitching arm past the hip. The pitcher may or may not take a step as the ball is delivered. If a step is taken, it may be forward or backward, as long as the pivot foot remains in contact with the pitcher's plate until the ball is released. In slow-pitch, the step need not be within the 24-inch width of the pitcher's plate.

Many slow-pitch pitchers back up after releasing the ball, some a few steps, others all the way to second base to plug up the middle. Remember, the deeper a pitcher plays, the more ground he can cover—also the more reaction time he has on a ball lined right back at him. As in fast-pitch, as soon as the ball is released, the pitcher becomes an infielder. And in slow-pitch, whether he backs up or not, he should anticipate that the ball will be hit hard right back at him (this is smart, just as a matter of self-defense). The disadvantage of backing up too far toward second is that the pitcher will not be able to cover first on a ball hit to the right side. If he knows that the batter regularly hits to the right side, he may want to back up only a stride or two, then get into a good defensive position. Some pitchers go back several steps if their pitch will have a low arc, and farther if their pitch will have a higher trajectory. A quick, sure-fielding pitcher allows the shortstop to cheat a step or two to his right, and the second baseman a step or two to his left. This can be a great advantage to a team's overall defense.

(Note: Depending on how far the pitcher backs up, he may have to drop to the ground to get out of the third baseman's or shortstop's way on a throw to first base.)

Pitching Strategy

The slow-pitch pitcher should proceed quickly from one pitch to the next to keep his teammates (and umpires) alert and on their toes. He should "talk it up" and remind players of the various defensive situations before the pitch is delivered. If the ball is hit to the outfield, he must back up the throw to the appropriate base. In fact, it is extremely important for the slow-pitch pitcher to be adept at backing up bases since there are so many hits. For all of these reasons,

FIGURE 8-7

FIGURE 8-8

FIGURE 8-9

***PITCHER BACKS UP AFTER
DELIVERY:*** *After releasing the
pitch, the pitcher backs up to get
into a defensive position to plug
up the middle.*

pitching in slow-pitch softball is a good position for an experienced player who is a leader.

It is critical that the pitcher adjust to each umpire's interpretation of the strike zone. Even well-qualified and experienced umpires have varying ideas of the strike zone. The pitcher must observe the umpire's calls and make any necessary adjustments. Remember, any pitch that hits the plate cannot be a strike. The batter's strike zone, as defined by the Amateur Softball Association's Official Playing Rules, is "...that space over any part of home plate between the batter's back shoulder and his knees when he assumes a natural stance." Umpires are supposed to call the strike zone as if the batter were directly at the plate. Moving up or back in the batter's box does not change the batter's strike zone. Many umps call balls and strikes by where the ball lands. Some draw an imaginary line from 12 to 24 inches or more behind the point of the plate. Pitches that land within that area and within the width of the plate are strikes. Pitches falling beyond the line are ruled deep, and are balls. Strikes must pass the corner of the plate where the triangular point begins. Most umps call a fairly large strike zone, knowing that slow-pitch is a hitter's game.

Many pitchers like to flirt with a 12½- or 13-foot pitch (or higher) early in the game to see how high a pitch the umpire will allow. It is not a good idea to throw successive high pitches, though, as umpires tend to be ready for the second one. In other words, if the ump lets a 13 footer go, don't throw the next one 14 feet high. Wait a few pitches, or until the next batter comes up, to throw a higher one. Pitchers often like to throw an illegal pitch (higher than 12 feet) on an 0-2 count, figuring they have nothing to lose. If the ump calls it illegal and the batter lets it go by, it will be a ball, bringing the count to 1-2. This can be considered a waste pitch. If the umpire doesn't call the pitch illegal, it may be called a strike, or the batter may swing at it. Another tactic is to throw short when ahead in the count, hoping to get the batter lunging after a low pitch that may hit the plate or bounce in front of it.

Although flat pitches (those with arcs closer to six feet) are easy to hit, in the right spot they can cause the hitter to get over-anxious and over-stride, resulting in a pop-up. Careful, though—it is important to avoid the long ball. Don't "lay the ball in the batter's wheelhouse."

The pitcher should try to get ahead in the count. Many slow-pitch players don't want to hit with two strikes and will swing at almost anything when behind 0-1. Avoid walks unless they are intentional, in which case the pitches don't have to be thrown. The pitcher just tells the umpire, "I want to put this batter on."

The easiest hitters to get out are those who crowd the plate. The toughest are those who stand away from it. If the batter is close to the plate, pitch him inside and deep. He will have trouble hitting this pitch to right field, and it will be difficult to hit hard and fair to left. If he is away from the plate, he is tougher to get out, but still pitch him a deep strike over the inside part of the plate. The toughest batter to pitch to is the one who is deep in the box and away from the plate. Pitch him on the outside part of the plate. If he is thrown an occasional short and inside pitch, he may overstride and pop-up or ground out weakly. In general, throw outside to the hitter who is looking to pull the ball and inside to the batter who wants to go the opposite way. Also, pitch short to batters who stand very erect, and deep to batters who crouch.

With a runner on first base, it is good strategy to pitch short, looking for a ground ball. With less than two outs a double play may develop. With a runner at second, try to get the hitter to hit the ball on the ground to the left side to keep the runner from advancing. Pitch short and inside to the righty, short and outside to the lefty. With a runner on third and less than two outs, throw short and inside—deep pitches can easily be hit to the outfield, allowing the runner to tag up and score.

IX. Running an Efficient Softball Practice

This chapter focuses on planning and organizing a practice around specific drills that make the most effective use of practice time. Please see Chapter I for detailed information on preworkout warm-up and stretching. Specific skills and techniques for fielding, hitting, etc., are covered in separate chapters and you may need to refer to them periodically. The chapters on Hitting, Throwing, Fielding, Baserunning, and Pitching all contain additional drills for developing technique.

Most softball practices are inefficient. This is true even of many high schools and colleges, whose coaches should know better. It is especially true of adult and youth summer-league teams. One player generally hits flies and ground balls and nine or more others stand around waiting for a ball to be hit their way. Or one player stands on the right- or left-field foul line hitting flies to the outfielders and another stands at home plate hitting grounders to the infield. Next comes batting practice, in which one guy bats and everybody else stands around hoping the ball gets hit their way. After an hour or so everyone heads for the beer coolers (adults) or Dairy Queen (youth leaguers) having had about a dozen swings and the same number of fielding chances.

Your practices may be infrequent and of short duration, so you must make the most of them, even if only a few of your players show up (an all-too-common occurrence with summer-league teams).

With a little advance planning, some well-structured drills, and a wristwatch, you can have a 60- or 90-minute practice that accomplishes a great deal. But you must be organized. Everything you do must be in the game plan, designed for a specific purpose and involving as many players at once as possible. For example, the following drills for infielders get everybody into the action. Each player is either an infielder, a fungo hitter (one who hits ground balls or fly balls), or a shagger (one who catches the ball for the fungo hitter). Used properly, these drills will get your players fielding a large number of ground balls in a very short time, making it one of the most efficient modes of fielding practice.

155

Multiple Ground Balls

Phase I

Instead of having one player alternate hitting to everybody on the field, have him stand on the first-base side of home plate and hit only to the third baseman. The third baseman fields the ball and throws it to a designated catcher (shagger) who positions himself next to the fungo hitter. Send a second batter and shagger about halfway down the line toward first base and have them hit balls to the shortstop. You now have six people active at once (two fielders, two fungo hitters and two shaggers). To get 12 people into the action, do the same thing on the other side of the diamond. One player on the third-base side of home plate hits to the first baseman, while another, halfway down the line toward third, hits to the second baseman. Each has his own shagger. The hitters, shaggers, and fielders can switch positions every so often, and a great many fielding chances can be handled in a short time. Extra players may fill in behind any infielder and alternate taking grounders.

Care must be taken with this drill, until the players get used to the set-up. It can be confusing, with balls being hit from all directions. You may find that this is compounded if some of your players are not very good fungo hitters. If slow rollers and toppers are being hit, say, to the shortstop, when he charges the ball to make the play, he will have to dodge a fungo from his right that's meant for the second baseman. Do not hit pop ups, fly balls, or bunts during this drill and tell the players not to charge slow rollers unless they're sure the coast is clear. Make sure everyone is alert to the possibility of players being in the line of fire and, after a short time, your unit will look like a precision drill team.

While many coaches have their outfielders, pitchers, and catchers relegated to hitting and shagging during this drill, we like to get everybody rotating and playing different positions. It is good for every player to field ground balls, no matter what position he regularly plays. Also, if you coach a summer youth team, your older players will occasionally miss games because they have to work, and even younger players will have other commitments. You are likely to use players at many different positions during the season.

One final note: It is a good idea for the coach *not* to hit fungoes or act as shagger. Instead, he should oversee the implementation of the drill and observe all the fielders and correct errors in fielding and throwing technique.

Phase II

This variation calls for two fungo hitters to alternate hitting ground balls. One hits to the third baseman who makes a throw to first base. Then a second fungo hitter (positioned half way down the line toward first) hits a ground ball to the shortstop who feeds the second baseman for an attempted double play. The two fungo hitters (each with his own shagger) must use good timing and coordinate their alternate hitting, making sure that the players are alert and ready. If any fielder is not involved in the action during the alternate play, he should get in the habit of cheering on his teammates who are making a play. This constant chattering is a sign of a hustling, "heads-up" team.

When done correctly, this drill is a picture of streamlined efficiency, with the third baseman working on fielding and making strong, accurate throws to first, the shortstop working on his "feeds" to the second baseman, the second baseman improving his double-play pivot, and the first baseman honing his footwork around the bag.

Phase III

In this phase the third baseman works on his double-play feeds to the second baseman, and the shortstop makes strong accurate throws to first. Again, the second baseman works on his pivot, this time with the throw coming from third. The first baseman continues to develop his footwork, properly shifting his feet around the bag (see Chapter V). The two fungo hitters must again alternate and use good timing to keep things moving, while making sure that players are ready when each fungo is hit.

Phase IV

Now the fungo hitters and shaggers move to the third base side of the diamond. One hitter, positioned near home plate, hits grounders to the first baseman who works on feeding the shortstop for a double play and, if he can, hurries back to take the return throw at first. If he cannot get back in time, the second baseman must cover (in a game situation, the pitcher may cover—communication as the play develops is essential). Alternately, the other fungo hitter, halfway down the line toward third, hits grounders to the second baseman who works on his feeds to the shortstop. The shortstop is perfecting his pivot and throw to first to complete the double play.

To keep the third baseman active, put a third fungo hitter and shagger on the first-base side of home plate and have him hit ground balls to third for a play at the plate.

Some things to remember: On double-play balls, get the pivot man in the habit of yelling "TWO! TWO! TWO!" to indicate to his teammate that a double play is in order. Infielders tend to rush throws on feeds to pivot men and pivot men to hurry their "turn." Tell them to take their time and get an out. The double play is a bonus. If you get it, fine—but you want that first out.

As umpires, we see this scenario almost every game: With a man on first, no outs and a ground ball to third, the third sacker senses the double play. He fields the ball cleanly and, in his exuberance, rushes his throw—throwing either before he is set, or before the second baseman gets near the bag. The ball ends up in right field and everybody advances an extra base. Now you have men on second and third with no outs and a potential for a big inning. A seasoned third baseman will take his time, be sure of the first out at second base, and end up with either a double play or a man on first with one out. If he doesn't get the twin killing, the double play and force play at second are still in order with the next batter. This "get an out" frame of mind is especially important for a team that is ahead in the score. If you're ahead, say, 6-0 in the sixth inning, you don't need a double play—one out will do just fine. (More on the mental side of softball in Chapter XI.)

Make sure your first baseman gives a chest-high target to all infielders throwing to him. Also, make sure your pivot man uses two hands on the pivot, not so much because he is less likely to drop the ball, but because it makes for a faster release. He doesn't have to reach into his glove with his throwing hand because it is already there, eliminating one needless motion.

Similarly, if an infielder boots a ground ball, have him "stay with it," executing every play as if it were a real game. "You play like you practice" is an old coaching adage. If he is in the habit of reacting quickly to a miscue and pouncing on the ball, he may still be able to get the out. But if his practice habits include hanging his head after misplaying a ball and kicking the dirt in disgust, he is likely to do the same in game situations. A player should always pick up a fumbled ball with his throwing hand and continue to make the play. If he picks the ball up with his glove, he will have to reach into the glove to transfer the ball to his throwing hand—another unnecessary motion.

Another way to handle an infielder's boot, if there is no longer any chance of retiring the runner, is to *occasionally* have your first baseman come off the bag toward the fielder, waving his arms and yelling "No, No, No!" to indicate no throw should be made. This gets the fielders in the habit of listening and communicating with each other. All too often a runner who was going to be safe at first anyway, ends up on second because the fielder makes an unnecessary, wild throw. The other infielders, who can look at the play and gauge whether or not an out can still be made, must communicate. Our experience is that players take too long in this decision-making. It takes a real "take charge" guy to watch a ball carom off a teammate's glove and immediately yell "You've still got 'em! You've still got 'em!" or "No play! No play!" (Some coaches prefer one-word communications, such as "One! One! One!" which means go ahead and throw to first, or "No! No! No!" which means swallow the ball, you'll never get the runner.)

Finally, all players should go through with all plays, making the proper throw to the proper base. The exception is if a double play is in order and a ground ball is booted, in which case the fielder must be alert to his teammates who may call out "One! One! One!" to indicate that the double play can no longer be made, so get an out at first. The runner from first is off on the pitch and has a running lead. But the batter must follow through with his swing and then start for first from a dead stop. This gives the fielder more time to retire the batter. So, even though the double play is muffed, a precious out can still be made.

You might spend five minutes on each of these four drills and accomplish a great deal in 20 minutes. Another variation is to have infielders doing these drills while outfielders, pitchers and catchers are doing drills specific to their fielding positions. The point is planning. A serious coach needs to make lesson plans just like any other teacher, and a coach is, after all, a teacher of sports. Be conscious of the time frame in which you must work, set up a schedule, and stick to it. As in other fields of learning, frequent short sessions are better than infrequent long sessions. Repetition is the key.

Batting Practice (BP in Softball Jargon)

Make a team rule that, whenever possible, all players must play their game-time positions during batting practice. An almost universal truth is that all outfielders want to be infielders, all infielders want to be pitchers, and all pitchers want to be hitters. So, if you let them, your players will be out of position during practice. Make them understand how valuable it is for ballplayers to get fielding chances *off the bat in game-like conditions*. This is not to diminish the importance of chasing fungoes. But balls coming off a hitter's bat during live pitching don't always behave as politely as fungoes. Hard hit balls can do all kinds of strange things—curve one way or the other, knuckle, sink, rise. This is especially true for balls hit to the outfield. Example: during live pitching, balls hit to right-field off the bat of a right-handed batter may tend to slice toward the right-field foul line. Similarly, balls hit to left field off the bat of a left-handed batter may curve toward the left-field line. Your outfielder may think he has a bead on the drive, but the more he runs, the more the ball moves away from him. Keep your players in their proper positions during BP, and they'll learn to track and run down these UFOs.

One of the reasons we don't see many great outfielders is that there aren't many great hitters. This is more true in fast-pitch softball and baseball than in slow-pitch softball. The problem is that in fast-pitch and baseball, the pitcher dominates the game (even in batting practice). That's because hitting is so tough. Even Ted Williams, who was arguably better at it than anyone who ever lived, says that hitting "…is the single most difficult thing to do in sport." Since so few batters consistently hit line drives and towering blasts, the outfielders don't get much chance to hone their fielding skills during live pitching (including BP). So, even when everyone plays his correct position during BP, batting practice can be boring and ineffective for the defensive-minded outfielder. There are some things a coach can do to remedy this. Following is a batting practice rotation that keeps everyone in the action.

Place all of your players in their correct position. Tell them to play every batted and thrown ball as if it were a game. Everyone must hustle into position, take relay throws, back up bases, etc. The trick here is to have an assigned task for each of the extra players and rotate so that everyone hits, and there are never more than the required number of players on the field at one time. If you have, say, three or four fielders in the same general area, they tend to congregate, tell stories, and socialize rather than take practice seriously. This creates a breeding ground for laziness and bad habits.

Let's say you have as many as 18 players at a practice (fast-pitch team). Send nine players to their positions, put a batter up at the plate (10), an on-deck hitter (11), a shagger for foul balls that go beyond the backstop or out of play (12), a first base coach (13), a third base coach (14), and the other four players can be baserunners.

There are a number of ways you can work with the extra baserunners. They might take turns running at first base. The fielders must be made aware of the situation, e.g., man on first, no outs, and play the batted ball accordingly. If the runner advances to third on a hit, he simply goes back to first and awaits his next turn to run. The runners practice their baserunning, getting a jump on the bases, listening and looking for base coaches and reacting to their instructions. You might place the runners on second or third or simultaneously at first and third or any other combination you want to practice.

Whatever the set-up, make a rotation. For example, one of the 18 players in the above illustration might rotate from his fielding position to third-base coach, to first-base coach, to the last of four baserunners, to the third of four baserunners, to the second baserunner, to the first baserunner, to shagger, to on-deck hitter, to batter and back to the field.

Again, try to keep outfielders in the outfield and infielders in the infield as much as possible during the rotation. Have someone assigned to count the batter's swings and get a new hitter every six swings. BP takes forever if you give each player too many swings—if it goes quickly with fewer swings, you might go around the rotation a second time.

To speed things up, you may want one of your players in the rotation shagging for the pitcher, that is, gathering and feeding softballs to the pitcher from a position between the pitcher and second base. For safety, make sure your pitcher doesn't pitch while the previous delivery is still being played (while infielders are looking up to field a high pop-up, for example).

There are a myriad of things extra players can be doing during BP. You might have a batting tee set up behind the backstop or you might have two players doing soft toss (see Chapter II) or other offensive or defensive drills. Again, a little planning goes a long way.

Note: If you play fast-pitch softball, have your pitchers pitch BP with a fast-pitch delivery. If you play slow-pitch, have them pitch BP with the same high arc that your hitters will face in games.

Other Modes of Batting Practice

Options for BP include varying the number of hits allowed each hitter (e.g., ten hits and four bunts (fast-pitch only) or six hits and two bunts). It always speeds things up if you allow a given number of *swings* rather than hits. The player who is feeding the pitcher should count. He should toss the ball to the pitcher when the pitcher is looking at him. The pitcher should not have to bend down to pick up balls—he is fed softballs and just keeps throwing pitches, one right after another, pausing only to make sure the fielders are ready. We tell our batting practice pitchers that they are well-oiled strike machines.

You might want to hit in groups of four players. Each group hits until all four players make one out. Then the next group comes in to hit, and the group that just batted goes to the field. You can keep score as in a game to add an element of competition to the drill (this always adds enthusiasm).

Another alternative batting practice makes use of stations to keep everybody active. For example, your stations may consist of three groups of five players each. At station one, a group hits live off a pitcher, while the second group hits whiffle balls off tees, and the third group practices bunting. You can add groups and stations such as soft toss, one-hand swings, etc. Groups rotate every five minutes.

Another popular batting practice is to have each player bat an entire bucket of balls. Place all the balls behind the pitcher's plate and then set the empty bucket out behind second base. The pitcher delivers one pitch after another, only waiting to be sure that the fielders are ready after each hit. Fielders toss any balls batted to them toward the bucket. When all balls have been hit, the players help refill the bucket, rotate to a new position, and BP continues. This is a good batting practice method for a short-handed team practice.

Yet another BP style is to give each batting team three outs in a game-like situation. Have nine players in the field and everybody else (hopefully six or fewer) up at bat. You may want to use two of the players to coach first and third. Each player stays up until he makes three outs. A force out that retires another runner counts as an out for the hitter. After three outs, clear the bases and start another inning. After a hitter makes three outs he goes on defense, and another player comes in to hit in his spot. To set a hustling tone throughout these BP sessions, call a hitter out if he is not ready to bat in a reasonable amount of time.

Modified Intra-squad Games

Another efficient way to combine BP with fielding is the modified intra-squad game. To speed things up and keep everyone active, play a game where each batter gets only one pitch. In other words, he comes to the plate with a 3-2 count. If the pitch is a ball, he walks; if it's a strike, he's out. Have the catchers call balls and strikes. The batter runs out any ball that he hits and the fielders make the plays, backing up bases, etc., as in a game. After three outs, any runners left on base should clear the bases and the team gets another three outs.

By playing six outs (two sets of three outs) you will have fewer offensive and defensive changes and this helps keep the game moving. If your catchers are using full catcher's gear, having two full sets available will streamline the switch from offense to defense.

Keep them hopping—they should sprint to their positions. Teams that don't hustle are likely to take three or more minutes between innings, locating their gloves, getting to their positions, warming up, etc. This makes for too much unproductive practice time.

Keep score during the intra-squad game and have each team's style of play reflect the game situation, the score, and the inning. Another way to play the intra-squad game is to have the batters come to the plate with a 2-2 count, giving them two chances to get a good ball to hit instead of one. Still another variation is to have a 1-2 count on the hitters. A good, informal way of keeping track of the batting order during these games is to bat by position. The pitcher bats first, followed by the catcher, first baseman, second baseman, third baseman, shortstop, left fielder, center fielder, right fielder and, in slow-pitch, the short fielder.

An interesting twist that can be used in these intra-squad games is to have each team at bat send their own pitcher to the mound to face his teammates. It is in his best interest, then, to give his teammate a good ball to hit. This results in more strikes being thrown, more balls being batted, and more fielding chances for everyone. The drawback is that the team in the field has no pitcher to help in calling out pop flies, backing up bases, covering first on balls hit to the first baseman, etc.

Another variation (useful when you don't have enough players for two full teams) is to have a full team of players in the field and three or four hitters at bat. Let the hitters bat and run the bases under game conditions, and stay at bat until their "team" makes three outs. Then they go to their respective positions and a new team of three or four batters comes to the plate.

Quick Tags

Many baserunners who should be tagged out in a game end up safe because of poor technique on the part of the would-be tagger. The most common error is not putting the tag down in front of the bag immediately. Many players hesitate, looking for the runner rather than dropping the glove straight down. Each fraction of a second of hesitation brings the runner closer to the bag. Too often the tag is brought down after a hesitation, and the glove strikes the player's knee while his foot is already touching the bag.

The following drill, which we designed and have used effectively for many years, is tailored to get players in the habit of making quick tags. They catch the ball and immediately place their glove in front of the bag that the runner is headed for.

Line up all your first basemen at first, your second basemen and shortstops at second, third basemen at third, and your catchers and pitchers at home. Outfielders can fill in at any base. One player in each line will be a thrower. He takes a position 20 or 30 feet away from his assigned base, where the angle from his throw will simulate a throw coming in from the direction of left field. He throws to each player in his line, who makes a catch and applies a quick tag without hesitating or looking for the runner. Taggers must position themselves so that they are not in the path of the oncoming, imaginary runner. The tagger returns the ball to the thrower and gets at the end of his line.

Change throwers every minute or so, and change the angle of the throws, too, so that they come from the direction of center field, right field, and the catcher (at this point the line at home plate will be taking throws from the backstop).

As a variation, have the baseman pretend that he has received the throw well ahead of the imaginary runner, giving him time to grasp the ball firmly in his throwing hand and to insert his hand and ball into the pocket of his glove while putting the tag down. A two-handed tag affords extra security that the ball will not be jarred loose.

Do not let the players make a sweep tag (where the glove and ball just briefly pass through the area of the bag). Have them place the glove on the ground directly in front of the bag. Some coaches feel that this increases the chance for injury, as the glove hand may be jammed between the slider's body and the bag. In fact, some umps will call the slider out *even without an actual tag* if the would-be sweep tag beats the slider to the base. These umps figure the fielder "pulled out early" only to protect himself from a needless injury and therefore shouldn't be penalized. Other umps will call "Safe!" on the same play, indicating, "Hey, this is softball, not the big leagues. You want an out, you gotta tag somebody." The safest bet is to make a quick tag, removing your glove hand as soon as the tag is made. Leagues that use breakaway bases or those that are not tied down have less to fear on this play.

Quick Tags and Bounce

We designed this variation of the quick tag drill when we noticed that many of our players, after making good quick tags, were oblivious to *other* baserunners advancing on the play. Players need to learn that their job is not done once they tag a man out (or he is ruled safe). They must immediately "bounce" around and check the other runner(s), being alert to the possibility of retiring a second (or third) runner on the same play.

Set your players up as in the quick tag drill but this time, after each tag is made, the tagger wheels around, takes the ball out of his glove and cocks his arm as if preparing to gun down an imaginary runner at another base. The coach yells out "Quick tag and bounce to third!," which means that after the tag everyone is checking the runner at third. The taggers at third will bounce to another base (e.g., home). Similarly, the coach might yell "Quick tag and bounce to second," in which case everybody bounces to second except the players who are already at second. They bounce to, say, third.

We try to get our taggers to wheel around by pivoting their bodies toward their *glove side*. For example, let's say a throw was coming in to second from right field. The right-handed shortstop is covering the base. After making the tag he begins his move to check the runner at third by pivoting his body *toward left field* rather than toward first base.

Quick Tags and Full Arm Fake

This is another useful variation of the quick tag drill. After making a quick tag and bouncing around to check another runner, the fielder makes a full arm fake. To perform this maneuver, the fielder keeps the ball in his glove and makes a hard, realistic-looking throw to another base *with his bare hand*. He shouldn't fake the throw with the ball in the throwing hand, as it may slip out of his control. Immediately after the full arm fake, the fielder wheels back and tags the imaginary runner who may have gone for the fake throw and come off the base.

The drill goes like this. The coach might call out "Quick tag and full arm fake to third." If the throw comes in from right field to second base, the fielder makes a quick tag, bounces glove side to third, fakes a throw (keeping the ball in his glove), and wheels back to tag the imaginary runner, now off the bag. We have seen this play work in games at all levels of play.

The final goal of these drills is to make the players' actions automatic. This takes many repetitions over a series of practice sessions, but eventually it all becomes one big reflex action.

Pop-ups and Fly Ball Drill (or Communication Drill)

This drill is not one of the most efficient, as it can lead to some standing around. However, it is so important that you must make time for it in your practice schedule. You will need at least one coach or player who can hit high pop-ups with some accuracy.

Put a full team of players in their regular positions, including a pitcher. Hit high infield pop-ups, trying to give every fielder some fielding chances (including the catcher). Try also to hit flies in the shallow outfield toward left, center and right field. This drill is for *communication*. Players must call for the ball loudly and clearly, yelling "I got it!" or the more grammatically correct "I have it!" (The older we coaches who still attempt to play get, the more likely we are to call out "I'll *try* it!") Generally, the pitcher should not field a pop-up unless he has to. Instead, he should help by calling out who *should* make the play. However, sometimes the pitcher is one of the team's best athletes. If so, you may want to encourage him to call for pop-ups. We have found it better to call a player's *position* rather than his name. This alleviates the situation where Bob lets the ball drop to the ground untouched because he thought you said Todd.

A critical role in the calling of pop-ups and fly balls is played by the *second* communicator. For example, if the shortstop and second baseman go behind second for a pop-up and the shortstop calls for the ball, the second baseman must communicate that he understood, calling "Shortstop, shortstop!" or something reassuring like "Okay, short, you have room!" We tell our players that it takes two or more people to communicate. One person can't do it alone.

You are likely to encounter two problems with the pop-up and fly ball drill. One is that players tend to take too long to make a call. Everybody will be staring up at the sky wondering who should play the ball, or hoping somebody else will play it. We tell our players to call it when the fly ball reaches its peak—sooner, if possible. If you call too early, someone else can still call you off, but when the call is late, no one is sure what will happen next. Ballplayers need to develop confidence in making these plays. They have to be take-charge types, leaders, which they will become with effective practices run by organized coaches.

The second problem that occurs during the Communication Drill is that two players call for the same ball at the same time. "I have it!, I have it!" yells the shortstop, loud and clear. "I got it! I got it!" screams the third baseman, equally assertive.

It is times like these when the pitcher should help out with the call. However, he may find his vocal cords mysteriously paralyzed and become a silent spectator, in which case one of the players has to take charge. It may be in the form of "No, No, No! I have it, get out of my way!" or it may be, "Okay third, you take it, you have lots of room." Communication—it takes two.

Some final notes on pop-up and fly-ball coverage: The center fielder should be the fastest runner and best defensive outfielder. He has *priority* on fly balls in the outfield. If he and another outfielder call for a ball at the same time, the other outfielder must give way to the center fielder. If you are using four deep outfielders (as opposed to three deep and one short fielder) in a slow-pitch game, the left center fielder has priority over the left fielder and the right center fielder has priority over the right fielder.

Similarly, all outfielders, including the short-fielder, have priority over all infielders. If an infielder, going back for a short fly ball hears an outfielder call for it, he should immediately give way to the outfielder. The play is generally easier for the fielder coming in than it is for the one going out. We tell our infielders to go after short flies to the outfield with reckless abandon *until they hear an outfielder,* then give way. If nothing is heard from an outfielder, it is the infielder's play all the way.

Pop-ups behind first base are often best handled by second basemen and pop-ups behind third are often easier for shortstops. Practice these often. Some coaches set up (and practice) a priority system for pop-up and fly ball coverage. This system rank orders each playing position in order of who should make the play when two or more players attempt to field the same fly ball. In a nine-player fast-pitch softball line-up, it would go as follows:

1. center fielder
2. left fielder/right fielder
3. shortstop
4. second baseman
5. third baseman
6. first baseman
7. pitcher
8. catcher

If you are using a short fielder (slow-pitch), he would be placed third on this list, moving the infielders and the battery down one place each. The short fielder, then, would have priority over the infielders but not over the other outfielders. Generally, high pop-ups are very tough plays for the catcher, so he has priority over no one. He should give way to *anyone* who calls for the ball.

Run-Downs

As umpires and coaches, we see run-downs botched more than just about any other play in softball. The following drill, if done correctly and regularly, will remedy your team's difficulties with this play.

Divide the team into two equal groups. Send one group out to work on run-downs between first and second, the other between third and home. Every player wears his glove, whether he is a runner or a fielder. Have an equal number of players at each base and, to

begin the drill, give a ball to the *second* man in line at one of the
bases. The first man in line will be the runner. When the player with
the ball yells "Go!" the runner takes off for the next base (he keeps
his glove on because he will be a fielder soon). He scrambles back
and forth between the bases in a "pickle" while the first players in
each line try to tag him out. After he is tagged out or safe at either
base, he gets at the end of the line (whichever line is closer). The
player who now has the ball (the tagger, if an out was made) tosses it
to the next man in line (whichever line is closer) and waits for the
"Go" signal, whereupon he sprints for the next base, trying to avoid
being tagged out. A great many run-downs can be practiced in a
short time, and we find this drill to be a good conditioner.

Points to emphasize: The player who yells "Go!" should hold the
ball in his throwing hand. He should cock his throwing arm, ready to
release the ball instantly. He must not be in a direct line with the
runner and his teammate, but he must get a couple of steps outside
(or inside) the baseline.

Let's say we have a right-handed first baseman starting the run-
down. He yells "Go!" and takes a position several steps toward right
field. His teammate at second should take a similar position (several
steps toward right-field). The first baseman sprints after the baserunner, attempting to catch up to him and tag him. He continues to hold
the ball in his throwing hand with his arm cocked, ready to release the
ball. He should avoid making repeated fake throws, as this may jar
the ball from his hand. If his teammate calls for the ball, yelling
"Now!" the first baseman gives him a quick, chest-high toss. The
move that makes or breaks this play is the timing of the call from the
receiver (it should be made when the runner is about 15 feet away)
and *his simultaneous movement toward the ball*. If the receiver
takes a step or two toward the thrown ball, he is likely to catch it and
tag the runner in one motion because the runner at this point is
stopping and trying to retreat in the opposite direction. If executed
properly, this procedure will retire the runner *with only one throw*.

This drill can be done in the outfield with as many lines as you like
(60 or 65 feet apart), but we believe the drill is safer in the infield
where overzealous baserunners won't be sliding on the grass (and
catching a spike in the turf). Also, the drill is more realistic when done
within the baselines. An important variation is the Run-Down and
Bounce Drill, where the fielder makes a tag and then wheels around
to check an imaginary runner at another base. If the run-down
involves many throws, each player making a throw may have to get
out of the baseline, as he is liable for *obstruction* if the runner bumps
into him in the baseline. The fielder may get out of the way and let the
next fielder in his line take his place.

To make things a little more game-like, some coaches like to start the run-down drill with a throw from a cut-off man positioned in the outfield. He throws the ball to second or first, which then initiates a run-down. (Or another cut-off man in left field throws the ball to third or home to start a third-base line run-down.) If the runner has not stopped between bases and is moving to a base, the cut-off man should throw the ball to whichever base the runner is going toward. If the runner is stationary between two bases, the player with the ball should sprint directly at him to force him to go to one base or the other. Let's assume a runner is stopped halfway between third and home, and the second baseman, who is the cut-off man in right field, has the ball. If the second baseman throws home, the runner will go back to third. If he throws to third, the runner will score. He must run at him, cutting the throwing distance down, and, when the runner commits to a base, gun him down. If the runner doesn't commit, the fielder should run right up to him and tag him out.

Short-handed Practice

If your softball team is like most teams, you may have some practice sessions when only a few players show up. Instead of complaining about the lack of enthusiasm or commitment, work with the players who do attend. With only four players you can have an excellent batting practice. You need only a pitcher, an infielder, an outfielder, and a batter. Using a large bucket of softballs works best. Dump the entire bucket of balls behind the pitcher's plate. As described earlier, place the empty bucket in a central location, such as the outfield, just beyond second base. The batter hits one ball after another and the fielders run down and toss the batted balls toward the bucket. Any ball fielded by the pitcher should be pitched again. When all of the balls have been batted, everyone helps refill the bucket, and the next hitter comes to bat. This is very efficient, giving everyone a great many swings and fielding chances in a short time. You may want to go around the rotation several times or work on other drills tailored specifically to the personnel you have present.

Sample 90-Minute Practices

The following are samples of efficient practice sessions, 90-minutes in duration. Use them as a guide. Put in any special plays or other points of emphasis you deem necessary. You may want to vary the drills or add some of your own. Use your imagination—be innovative. Make up drills that fill any need that arises with your team—this is how we developed drills like our Quick Tags, Quick Tags and Bounce, and Quick Tags and Full Arm Fake. Remember to repeat drills on different occasions. Don't let your players just "go through the motions" during drills. Make sure they understand how each relates to what's going to happen in games. When we are coaching in a game and see the ball coming in to a base and our player about to catch it and tag a runner, we yell out "Quick Tag!" to remind him to put the glove straight down without hesitating—just like in practice. When we see a man caught between two bases and our player with the ball, we yell out, "Run-down!" to remind him to make the play just like we worked on it in practice.

A team's success is related to two major factors: how talented the players are, and how well organized and meaningful the practices are. You need a lesson plan with clear-cut goals for each practice, a time schedule, and the discipline to keep to your schedule. Good planning, repetition and proper technique are the keys.

Practice I

6:00-6:05 Jog
6:05-6:15 Stretch and throw
6:15-6:20 Multiple Ground Balls—Phase I
        (players throw hard only after arms are well warmed up)
6:20-6:25 Multiple Ground Balls—Phase II
6:25-6:30 Multiple Ground Balls—Phase III
6:30-6:35 Multiple Ground Balls—Phase IV
6:35-6:38 Quick Tags
6:38-6:43 Run-Downs
6:43-6:48 Two-Ball Drill
6:48-6:53 Range Drill
6:53-6:58 Angle-Back Drill
6:58-7:00 Water Break
7:00-7:10 Communication Drill
7:10-7:30 Batting Practice

Practice II

6:00-6:05 Jog
6:05-6:15 Stretch and throw
6:15-6:20 Pepper
6:20-6:23 Four Square
6:23-6:26 Multiple Ground Balls—Phase II
6:26-6:29 Multiple Ground Balls—Phase III
6:29-6:32 Multiple Ground Balls—Phase IV
6:32-6:35 Quick Tags and Bounce

6:35-6:39 Run-Downs
6:39-6:54 Infielders fungo and shag for outfielders who work on
    Liner, Shallow, and Do or Die Drill, five minutes each
    (pitchers and catchers work on pitcher/catcher drills)
6:54-7:00 Situation practice—fastpitch teams work on bunt de-
    fenses, slowpitch teams work on relays and cut-offs
7:00-7:30 Modified Intra-Squad Game, 3-2 count, six outs

Practice III

6:00-6:05 Jog
6:05-6:10 Stretch and throw
6:10-6:17 Baserunning
6:17-6:37 Infielders do Multiple Ground Balls—Phases I to IV;
    outfielders do four outfield drills at five minutes each
6:37-6:40 Quick Tags and Full Arm Fake
6:40-6:43 Run-Downs
6:43-6:45 Run-Downs and Bounce
6:45-6:52 Mass Bunting (fast-pitch teams); game situations (slow-
    pitch teams)
6:52-6:54 Water break
6:54-7:10 Hitting stations
7:10-7:30 Modified Intra-Squad Game (2-2 count, six outs)

Note: Coaches should allow a two or three minute "water break" to
allow the athletes to replace fluids lost through sweating. This is very
important, especially on warm, humid days.

Following the Lead of Major College Coaches

This chapter really takes a page out of the top level college (and
high school) coaches' practice book. Everything is "on the clock," a
couple of minutes for this, three minutes for that. Drills are designed
to keep everybody active—no standing around. You may want to get
permission from your local high school and college coaches to
observe their practices. Even baseball practices can be helpful to
watch, as many of the drills can be adapted for fast-pitch or slow-
pitch softball.

When you run well-organized, efficient practice sessions, you'll
inspire confidence in your players. They'll respect you for the
planning time and effort you put in; they'll believe in you; they'll
believe in themselves. They'll become winners.

X. Team Defense

Mental Aspects of Team Defense

A solid team defense should strive to issue no walks and commit no errors. The pitcher and other defensive players must concentrate on retiring the lead-off hitter each inning. When the lead-off hitter reaches base, his team has a good chance of scoring at least one run.

We almost never play "infield in" to cut a run down at the plate. As we have stated earlier, the deeper you play the more ground you can cover. You must balance this truth with the possibility of a bunt in fast-pitch softball. When you play infield in, you increase a hitter's batting average by reducing your fielders' range. A ground ball that may have been an out, becomes a base hit and the opponents have a big inning instead of scoring one run. It is better defensive strategy to play back and avoid the big inning. Always play deep when no one is on base and any time there are two outs. Also, play deep when you are ahead by many runs, even with a runner on third. Give up the run in exchange for an out.

We do play infield in when one run will hurt us in the late innings (runner on third, second and third, or first and third, with the lead runner an important run). We position the first and third basemen even with the bag, and the second baseman and shortstop a couple of steps in back of the baseline. An infielder should never throw the ball to the catcher for a close play at the plate at the expense of a sure out elsewhere unless he is trying to retire the go-ahead run late in the game.

With the bases loaded and less than two outs, we like to have the first and third basemen play even with the bag and play for a home-to-first double play, while the middle infielders stay at double-play depth and go for a second-to-first double play. With more experienced players, you may want to practice this option on the traditional double play: With first and second or bases loaded, get an out at second and then throw to third to try to catch a careless runner rounding the bag. This is good strategy when the batter is a fast runner and/or the ball is batted slowly, reducing the chances of a conventional twin killing.

Slow-pitch infielders especially should play deep since there is no threat of a bunt or steal. Some strong-armed infielders like to play several steps out on the outfield grass. If your infielders are consistently throwing runners out by 10 to 15 feet, they are playing too shallow. The first baseman should play as deep as he can and still get to first in time to cover on a throw from an infielder.

While we like our infielders deep, we prefer our outfielders to play somewhat shallow. We work hard at teaching our outfielders to go back for drives so that we can play in and catch batted balls that would otherwise go for singles. Of course, we back them up for the other team's power hitters, and we often play them deeper in the late innings of a close game, preferring to give up a single over an extra-base hit. We especially like our right fielder to play shallow on right-handed hitters and our left fielder to play shallow on left-handed hitters. Not many batters hit to the opposite field with power, and many hitters, particularly in fast-pitch, swing late, inadvertently slapping bloopers to the opposite field. In any case, youth-league outfielders need to learn to get the ball into the infield immediately after making a play on a ground or fly ball. Too many hold the ball in the outfield, allowing alert baserunners to advance.

Most top-caliber slow-pitch teams use four outfielders across rather than three and a short fielder. The short fielder usually just catches an occasional liner right at him or short pops that the second baseman or shortstop might get to anyway. With four outfielders it is advisable to be very aggressive in chasing short flies and liners as someone will be backing up (careful on drives down the left- and right-field lines though—these are tougher to back up).

Recently, we saw this heads-up play by a right fielder: With one out and a runner at first, he called for a short fly beyond second base even though he knew neither he nor the second baseman could get to it. He decoyed the runner at first into going halfway, caught the ball on the bounce, and retired him at second on a force out.

Consider *not catching* a deep foul ball with an important run on third base and less than two outs, as the runner may tag and score after the catch. This is especially important in slow-pitch because of the third-strike rule (you are out if you hit a foul ball with two strikes). The batter is out, but if the foul is a caught fly ball, the ball is live and runners may advance after the catch. It is to the defense's advantage to let the foul fall untouched, retiring the batter, and preventing the advance of other baserunners. Similarly, when a runner is in a position to tag and score, consider not catching foul balls while moving away from the plate (e.g., the first baseman running with his back to the plate for a foul pop beyond first base). This is a tough play, requiring the fielder to catch the ball, bring his momentum under control, turn, and throw to the plate. If you are ahead by several runs in any of these situations, make the catch and take the out.

Making the Double Play

Whenever there is a runner on first and less than two outs, the pitcher must know which middle infielder will be covering second on a grounder back to the pitcher's plate, so he won't have to play a guessing game when he fields the ground ball. He can watch the appropriate fielder get into position and confidently make a strong throw to him. It is important for the pitcher (or any fielder) not to rush this throw, especially when you are ahead. If you are ahead by six runs, you don't need a double play—you just need an out. The double play would be a bonus. Teach your players to get into the "get an out" frame of mind. In a seven inning game, a team bats for 21 outs. Every time you retire a runner, the offense has one less out at its disposal.

On double play balls near second base let the middle infielder (if he is reasonably close to the bag) take the double play himself. The fewer people who handle the ball, the less chance of errors and, with most youth leaguers, the faster the release of the ball to first base.

Pick-offs (Fast-Pitch Only)

Unless you have a talented defensive unit, use pick-offs sparingly. They can backfire easily, leading to a big inning for the offense. Of course, along with the risk is the possibility of great reward. Pick-offs sometimes work best in critical situations. They are also worth trying when your pitcher is struggling.

The most successful pick-offs are at first base. The catcher signals a pitch-out (a fastball out of the strike zone). The first baseman moves in toward home plate (where the runner can see him), as if anticipating a bunt. The second baseman then sneaks in behind the runner, taking a snap throw from the catcher, and putting a quick tag down. Pick-offs are often successful after a missed bunt attempt, catching a careless runner moving or leaning the wrong way.

With younger or less-talented players you may want to have the first baseman anchor at first to take the throw, with the second baseman and right fielder backing up. If your purpose with the attempted pick-off is only to keep a runner close to his base, a safer play is to have your catcher make a fake throw.

Pick-offs at second are less successful because of the long throw from the catcher and the possibility of an alert baserunner advancing to third on the throw. Sometimes a careless runner can be picked off by the pitcher, who, after getting the ball back from the catcher, wheels and throws to the second baseman or shortstop. This throw should be waist-high and to the third-base side, allowing an easier quick tag.

For pick-offs at third, the third baseman can cover with the shortstop backing up. Like the first base pick-off, the third baseman can play in to decoy the runner and the shortstop can sneak in behind. Again, this requires a predetermined signal and a pitch-out.

When there are two or more runners on base, consider picking off a trail runner, who often feels he is safe because the defense is more concerned with the lead runner. Careful though—a mistake can be costly.

The Intentional Walk

Sometimes it is good strategy to walk a batter on purpose. You may want to avoid pitching to an excellent hitter, a power hitter, or one who is on a hot streak. Or you may want to set up forced outs by walking a batter with a runner at second or runners at second and third. (This also increases your chances for a double play.) An intentional walk can take away your opponents' option to try the squeeze play, as most teams won't squeeze with the bases loaded because of the force out at the plate.

In slow-pitch softball, the pitcher need not throw the pitches on an intentional walk. He simply notifies the plate umpire of his intention and the batter automatically takes first. Slow-pitch prohibits stealing and advancing on passed balls or wild pitches, so throwing the pitches during an intentional walk makes no sense.

Since those possibilities do exist in fast-pitch, the pitcher must deliver the pitches. He should throw well outside the strike zone, and the catcher should stand up and extend his throwing arm to the side to indicate an intentional walk. The catcher must stay in the catcher's box until the pitch is released, then quickly move outside to catch the pitch. The pitcher must be careful not to pitch too close to the plate, or an aggressive hitter will rip the ball to the opposite field.

In slow- or fast-pitch, you may want to consider throwing the batter four very bad pitches, hoping he will swing at one and pop up or ground-out weakly. We like to intentionally walk the batter when runners are at second and third with less than two outs—especially if this lets us "pitch around" a good hitter.

If there is a double in the last half of the last inning and one run will beat you, intentionally walk the batter. If the hit is a triple, walk the bases loaded. The idea is to set up force outs so that your fielders have more chance to retire the side without the lead runner scoring. Since one run wins the game anyway, the extra baserunners don't really hurt you. There are a few things to consider before employing this strategy: Can your pitcher throw strikes when he has to, even after giving up intentional walks? Are the hitters that you are bypassing weaker batters than the ones you are pitching to? Like any strategy, if it works, the manager is a genius—if it backfires, he's a bum!

Bunt Defense (Fast-Pitch Only)

When defending the bunt with a runner on first only, we have our first and third basemen charge hard (but under control) to the plate. The shortstop covers second and the second baseman covers first. If the third baseman fields the ball, the catcher or pitcher covers third base to prevent the runner from going all the way to third. If the third baseman doesn't field the ball, he must immediately go back to cover third.

While the pitcher, first baseman, or third baseman field the ball, they listen for instructions from their teammates, especially the catcher, who is facing the field and can see the runner. He must look at the runner and make a quick decision, telling his teammate where to throw the ball ("One! One! One!" for first base and "Two! Two! Two!" for second base). Always get an out on a bunt. If not the lead runner, any runner. Only go for the lead runner if you are sure you can get him out. When making his quick decision, the catcher must consider the score of the game, as well as where the ball is bunted and how hard it is bunted. If the ball is bunted hard right back to the pitcher, it should be an easy out at second. If your team is ahead by several runs, don't take a chance at second, take the sure out at first.

Another defensive option is to anchor the first baseman and have the pitcher cover bunts on the first-base side. The second baseman covers second and the shortstop covers or backs up third. In either case, you may want to get your fielders in the habit of throwing to second after an out at first to try and catch a runner rounding the bag. On all bunts the outfielders must back up their appropriate base (left fielder backs up third, center fielder backs up second, and right fielder backs up first).

To defend a bunt with runners at first and second, we like to "anchor" the third baseman, sending the pitcher to cover the bunt on the third-base side. If the ball is bunted hard right at the third baseman, we tell him to listen to his teammates and, unless they call for a play at third, make the play to first base.

When defending against the bunt with runners at first and third, we have our shortstop cover third, looking for a possible throw to catch the lead runner. The play is most likely to go to home, third, or first. The squeeze play is not as effective in fast-pitch softball as it is in baseball, since a runner can't leave his base until the pitch is released. Nevertheless, it is employed, can be effective, and must be defended. If you suspect a squeeze and the count is in your favor, you can pitch out. In all bunting situations, it is a good idea to throw high strikes. These are tough to bunt and are often popped up. If the pitcher or other player fields a squeeze bunt, he should throw a low underhand or backhand toss to the catcher. Again, the shortstop covers third on the attempted squeeze if there are trail runners.

As in other facets of play, you must practice bunt defenses enough to build confidence and to take the uncertainty out of your players' actions, and reactions. Consider the count before calling pitch-outs on suspected bunts or pick-offs. Can you afford for the pitch to be called a ball if the play does not develop as you anticipated?

Bunt Defense Drill

Put your fielders in position with runners at home plate and first base. The coach stands at the plate with a ball and the pitcher has a second ball. Notify your infield of the bunt situation (e.g., runner at first, no outs). The pitcher delivers a pitch to the plate and, when the catcher receives it, the coach rolls his ball out on the field as if it were bunted. (The catcher drops the pitched ball and plays the one rolled out by the coach.) The fielders and baserunners play the bunt as they would in a game. After a play, the ball is returned to the pitcher for the next pitch and bunt. After a player runs from home, he goes to the end of the line at first, and the runner from first goes to the line at home. Throw a pop-up occasionally to teach your runners not to advance until the bunted ball is on the ground. Next, put runners at first and second, first and third, etc., and drill them on all facets of bunt defense.

Defending Against First and Third Double Steals (Fast-Pitch Only)

There are a number of baserunning options for the offense with runners at first and third. The runner at first can attempt a steal, hoping that the catcher will throw to second, thereby allowing the runner from third to scamper home. Some teams will just let the stealer go, rather than risk a throw. To force the defense's hand, the stealer may stop halfway between the bases or retreat toward first. This may be legal depending on the situation—remember, once the ball is in the pitcher's possession within the circle, the runner must go back to his base or proceed to the next base, or he will be declared out. Whenever a first and third double steal is in progress, we tell our players to throw the ball to second base. It just doesn't seem like sport to us to concede a base to a runner without even attempting to retire him. However, our catcher checks the runner at third as he is setting to throw to second. If he sees that the runner from third is advancing home or is well off the base, he aborts the throw to second, and plays on the runner at third (he may make a fake throw to second before playing on the runner at third).

The catcher must throw low and hard, when throwing through to second base, and then be prepared for a return throw from one of the middle infielders. We have one infielder take the throw (usually the shortstop) and another act as a cut-off man (usually the second baseman) about 10-15 feet in front of second. As the throw is in flight, the cut-off man checks the runner at third. If he breaks for home, the cut-off man moves toward the ball, catches it, and fires it to the plate. If the runner is well off third but not headed for home, the cut-off man meets the ball and throws to third. The other fielders can help the cut-off man by yelling "Home!" or "Four!" as soon as the runner breaks for home. If the runner is holding at third and not too far off the bag, the cut-off man lets the throw go through to the base, and the fielder there makes a quick tag.

As a general rule, once the cut-off man lets the ball come through to second, the other fielder should forget about the runner at third, and get an out at second. The cut-off man must be careful not to screen the other fielder's view, as injury can result. If the shortstop has a stronger arm than the second baseman, or is a better all-around player, we may have him take the cut-off, and the second baseman cover the bag. There is a trade-off here as the shortstop has a tougher angle, having to look back over his shoulder to see the runner at third.

Another way to defend against the first and third double steal is to have your best middle infielder play a step in front of second and, if the runner at third holds, he receives the throw from the catcher and tags the runner at second. If the runner from third breaks for home, he moves quickly toward the ball, catches it, and fires a strike to the plate. The other middle infielder backs up the throw to second.

Another option for the offense in this situation is to have the runner at first take off just as the catcher releases his throw back to the pitcher (there is an element of surprise to this strategy, called a delayed steal). To discourage delayed steals, the catcher should check the runner before throwing to the pitcher, even faking a throw to keep the runner close to the base. If a delayed steal does occur, the pitcher can wheel and throw to second. If the runner from first slows down, stops, or retreats, the fielder with the ball can see both runners, and make a decision about which runner to play on. With two outs we usually play on the runner at first, as a quick out will retire the side. Careful though—if the runner from third touches home before the third out is made, the run counts.

Another option for the defense is to have the pitcher just hold the ball in the 8-foot circle. Now the runners must return to their bases or proceed to the next base. This restriction is off if the pitcher leaves the circle or makes a play, including a fake throw, on the runner. A variation that we like to use when the runner from first is walking toward second, trying to draw a throw, is to have our pitcher move out of the circle toward the runner. The runner at third usually thinks that the pitcher's attention is diverted, and he breaks for home. We have our pitcher take several steps toward second and wheel around quickly. Often, he catches the runner breaking for home or stranded too far off third. In either case, the runner can be picked off easily with a good throw. If the runner at third is stopped between third and home, the pitcher should run at him to force him to commit to one base or the other.

A defense of the first and third steal that works with very young or overanxious baserunners is to have the catcher throw the ball directly to the pitcher. The pitcher catches the ball and throws the runner out at third or home, if possible. The catcher's throw must look like a legitimate throw to second to fool the runner at third (a high throw makes the best decoy).

Sometimes a steal is initiated by drawing a pick-off throw from the catcher. The runner at first takes a long lead after the pitch, trying to draw a throw from the catcher. If the catcher throws, the runner takes off for second or intentionally gets in a run-down. To prevent this, have your catcher make fake throws to first and/or get the ball right back to the pitcher in the circle.

Yet another way the double steal can be initiated is by the batter receiving ball four with a runner on third. The batter simply keeps going to second after touching first, either running or walking, trying to provoke the defense into playing on him. Whenever a runner breaks for the next base, the fielder who reads it first must yell "there he goes!" to alert his teammates. Once the runner heads for second, the defense is the same as above—have the pitcher hold the ball in the circle, throw it to a middle infielder, or take several steps and wheel.

Cut-offs

Cut-offs are used to intercept a throw to a base. Once a throw is cut off, a play can be made on another runner. For example, for plays at home-plate, some coaches designate the first baseman as the cut-off player for all fields, while others make him the cut-off player on balls hit to left-center, center, right-center, and right-field, and make the third baseman take the cut-off from left-field. Some coaches (at lower levels especially) use the pitcher as the cut-off player. For plays at the plate, the cut-off player should position himself about 30 feet from home. The catcher gives instructions to the cut-off player, lining him up by indicating "right, right" or "left, left", or "okay, okay". The idea is to make a straight line between the outfielder, cut-off player, and the base. The cut-off player must be ready to react quickly to a bad throw. The catcher calls "Cut-hold" (cut the throw and hold onto it), "Cut-2" (cut the throw and toss to second), "Cut-3" (cut the throw and toss to third), or "Relay" (cut and throw to home). If he says nothing, the cut-off man should let the ball go straight through to the base. If the cut-off man has to cut the ball and make a throw, he should turn glove side when possible, crow hop, and throw.

Relays

Relays are necessary when balls are hit so deep that two short throws are more effective than one long throw, such as when the ball is hit into the gap between two outfielders or over an outfielder's head. The shortstop goes out for the relay if the ball is hit to left- or center-field, and the second baseman takes the relay position if the ball is hit to right-field. The middle infielder not taking the relay covers second base, helps align the relay player, and tells him where to throw the ball. If it becomes obvious that no play will be made at second, he goes out to back up the relay or, in some cases, acts as a double relay. The relay player runs into the outfield and assumes a position that creates a straight line between him, the outfielder, and the base to which the ball will be thrown. He can look over his shoulder to check the progress of the runner. Also, he should gauge his distance so that the outfielder makes the longer of the two throws (two-thirds the distance versus one-third the distance). The relay player should wave his arms vigorously, yelling "Hit me! Hit me!" to help the outfielder find the target. The outfielder should throw overhand at the target's chest. The relay player catches the ball with two hands, turns glove side, crow hops, and throws. A good relay player receiving an accurate throw can speed up his release by starting his crow hop just before he catches the ball. The relay throw should be low and hard, coming in to the base on a hop (or two). Like a cut-off player, a relay player must be ready to react quickly to a bad throw. Whenever he is told by his teammates to hold the ball, he should run it into the infield.

The best way to practice cut-offs and relays is to hit fungoes with men on base and fielders in their positions. Have runners breaking from home plate, too. Make the defense react according to where the ball is batted. Hit sure doubles down the left- and right-field lines as well as drives in the outfield gaps.

Competitive Relay Drill

Set up equal lines of relay players in the outfield (three groups of five, or four groups of four) parallel to each other and running from the left-field line to deep center-field. Spread the players out—the spacing will depend on the age and ability of the players (anywhere from 60 to 90 feet apart). The first player in each line has a ball. On the coach's whistle, the first players throw to their respective relay players who catch, turn, and throw to the next relay players in line until the balls get to the end of the line. If any ball is overthrown, the team must get it back to the player who should have caught it and continue from there. Players should wave their hands high overhead and yell "Hit me! Hit me!" All throws should go to the relay player's glove side so that he can catch, turn, and throw to the next player quickly. Play continues until the ball gets back to the original man. The first line to accomplish this is the winner. A variation of this drill is to require the ball to go around twice or three times.

XI. Offensive Strategy

All of the offensive strategy discussed below involves taking a gamble. We like to keep the pressure on the defense by employing daring strategy. If you practice the procedures well, you are likely to find that they are not so risky in the long run.

The Steal (Fast-Pitch Only)

The steal is probably the most potent weapon in a youth team's offensive arsenal. Few teams have catchers who can make quick, accurate, strong throws. Many youth leagues prohibit stealing because they cannot defend against it successfully. If the opponents' catcher does throw well, we recommend stealing when the score is close or when you are ahead. Of course, the speed and baserunning ability of your baserunner is a major consideration.

A team should fake steal occasionally. To do this, the runner breaks from the bag as he would on a steal, but pulls up quickly, squaring up to the infield and reading the ball. A fake bunt during a steal attempt keeps the catcher back a little longer and gives the baserunner an extra edge. Also, a left-handed batter obstructs the catcher's view of an attempted steal. Some coaches have the batter swing to miss if he has no strikes on him (or fake a bunt) to keep the catcher back a fraction longer. While attempting a steal, the runner should use the peek technique described in Chapter VI. With runners at first and second the double steal is an effective maneuver. Both runners break on the release of the pitch.

With runners on first and third there are a number of effective stealing maneuvers open to you. The idea is to try to get the defense to play on the runner attempting to steal second base so that the runner on third can score. As outlined in the previous section on defending against these plays, the options are:

1. *Straight steal:* The runner from first breaks when the pitch is released. If the catcher throws through to second, the runner from third attempts to score. The runner from third should not go until the ball is past the pitcher, as he may cut the throw off.

2. *Delayed steal:* The runner at first breaks as soon as the ball leaves the catcher's hand on his return throw to the pitcher. The runner at third reads the play as it develops, and scores if the opportunity presents itself.

3. Delayed steal off an attempted pick-off: The runner at first takes a long lead after the pitch is released to induce the catcher to attempt a pick-off at first base. If the catcher throws to first, the runner goes to second.

4. Steal off ball four with a runner on third. After walking to first, the batter continues on to second. Often on this play, the ball comes back to the pitcher in his circle before the batter-baserunner reaches first. If this is the case, the batter-baserunner is allowed to stop or hesitate and then immediately go one way or the other. (A second stop or hesitation will make him automatically out.) If the pitcher makes a play on the runner, including a fake throw, the restriction about going one way or the other is off. Once a runner returns to a base, he may leave the base again only if a play is made on him or another runner, the pitcher loses possession of the ball, the pitcher leaves the 8-foot circle, or he makes another pitch.

In any of the above plays, the trail runner may elect to walk, stop, or retreat toward first to provoke the defense into playing on him (pay attention to the restrictions described above). With two outs, you may want him to stay in a rundown until the runner from third crosses the plate. This is particularly good strategy with two outs and a weak hitter at the plate, or any time a run is crucial to you. Use your imagination and come up with other offensive maneuvers. For example, with less than two outs and a pop-up in the infield, have the runner at first tag up after the catch and walk or sprint to second.

The Sacrifice Bunt (Fast-Pitch Only)

With a successful sacrifice bunt, your chances of scoring one run go up, but your chances of a big inning go down. So, we suggest you sacrifice bunt any time one run is important to you. The sacrifice may be used with a runner at first, or runners at first and second with less than two outs. We even like to bunt our better hitters if the situation dictates it. We also like to play for one run early in the game. We want to get ahead because this often changes our opponents' strategy. With runners on first and second and no outs, we even sacrifice our best hitter, if the score is close. There are a great many ways you can score from third with one out in fast-pitch softball. Try to keep the bunt away from the pitcher and toward first or third base.

Fake Bunt and Slash (Fast-Pitch Only)

The fake bunt and slash is good strategy with a runner on first only, or runners on first and third. We like our players to pivot on both feet (see Chapter II for this technique), show the bunt early, and then try to hit the ball on the ground past a charging infielder. If there is a runner on first, this can be executed while the baserunner is stealing.

Hit-and-Run (Fast-Pitch Only)

It is best to attempt the hit-and-run with a runner on first base and a hitter with excellent bat control at the plate. The number of outs is not a factor. The hit-and-run is effective when the hitter is ahead in the count (2-0, 3-1, or 3-2) and a fastball can be expected. The runner on first breaks for second on the pitch, and the hitter tries to hit the ball on the ground anywhere, but especially behind the runner or through the area left vacant by the middle infielder moving to cover second. The hit-and-run generally is used when the baserunner is *not* a speedy base-stealer. Therefore, to protect the runner, the hitter should swing if the pitch is anywhere near the strike zone. The hit-and-run can also be employed with runners on first and third—the runner on third does not steal on the pitch.

If the runner at first *and* the batter are slow baserunners, and there are less than two outs, the hit-and-run may help you avoid a double play. Again, you must have a good contact hitter at the plate.

Run-and-Hit (Fast-Pitch Only)

The run-and-hit is similar to the hit-and-run except that the baserunner needs good speed and must be a threat to steal. The batter will still swing at a strike and try to hit behind the runner, but he can take a pitch that is not to his liking because the runner needs no protection. Both the hit-and-run and the run-and-hit will result in the batter reaching first, and the runner advancing two bases, if they are well-executed.

Run-and-Bunt (Fast-Pitch Only)

The run-and-bunt can be used with a runner on first or second, or runners at first and third. The idea is to try to advance two bases on the bunt. The runner on first or second takes off when the pitch is released. If the pitch is a strike, the batter executes a drag bunt or a sacrifice bunt; if not, the runner steals the base. If the runner is on first, the batter should bunt to the third baseman, increasing the likelihood that third will be left uncovered.

Baserunners should always use the peek technique and listen to base coaches. This way they will know if the ball was popped up, in which case they must attempt to get back to base immediately or they'll be doubled up. The same counts that are suggested for the hit-and-run are good for the run-and-bunt.

Bunt-and-Run (Fast-Pitch Only)

The bunt-and-run is used when the runner is not a good base-stealer. The hitter must try to bunt any decent pitch to protect the runner. You send the runner on the pitch, but more to set him in motion than to steal the base. Again, attempt this play when the count is such that the pitcher needs to throw a strike.

Squeeze Bunt (Fast-Pitch Only)

The squeeze bunt (often called the suicide squeeze) is effective with a runner at third, runners on second and third, or runners at first and third. Both runners break when the pitch is delivered, and the batter attempts to bunt the ball no matter where the pitch is. Often the trail runner can advance two bases if the bunt is well executed, and the ball is thrown to first. The squeeze can be more effective with a right-handed batter, as this blocks the catcher's view. In any case, the batter must be an excellent bunter.

It is not a good idea to squeeze bunt with the bases loaded because an out at any base is a force out, and, when the third out of the inning is a force out, no runs may score on the play. Sometimes a squeeze play backfires because someone misses the signal. The runner takes off from third, sprints hard to the plate, only to run into the catcher with the ball, ready to tag him, because the batter didn't get the signal. Since it is essential that both the bunter and the baserunners know that the squeeze play is on, we have them acknowledge our signal. After we give the squeeze signal, the batter and runner(s) pick up dirt and toss it to the ground. This tells us that everybody has the signal straight.

The safety squeeze is an alternate way to bunt a run home. The runner from third breaks for the plate only if a good bunt is put down, or after the ball is fielded and thrown to first.

Signals

The trick with giving signals is to make them appear complicated even though they are simple. In many cases, we aren't that concerned if the defense knows what is coming. They still have to execute proper defensive technique to stop it. Use one item or part of the body as the indicator. When the coach touches this, it indicates that a signal is coming. The first thing touched after the indicator is the signal. For example, let's say that your signal for the bunt is the belt. The coach touches his face, arms, stomach, etc., in random order. He then touches his cap, followed by his belt. All of the parts of the body or objects touched before the cap are just decoys. Once the cap is touched, the signal follows. To make it harder for the defense to steal your signals, the coach should continue to give decoy signals after the real one is communicated, and the players should not turn away until the coach completes this series of signals. We usually clap our hands to indicate that we are done signalling. (If you think that the defense has stolen your signals, you can change the indicator.)

Selecting the Batting Order

There are a number of different ideas about selecting a proper batting order. One says that you should bat your best hitter first and second-best hitter next, all the way down to the weakest hitter. The idea is that the best hitters will come to bat more often.

Most coaches put the player with the highest on-base percentage first in the line-up. He makes the fewest outs and is usually a speedy, heads-up baserunner. In slow-pitch, he is a player who hits very few fly balls.

The number-two hitter is a batter who can move runners around. He can hit to the right side and is a fast runner who avoids double plays. This is a good spot for a left-handed hitter who is a couple of steps closer to first than a righty. He hits for average, and, in fast-pitch, is a good bunter.

The number-three hitter is the best hitter on the team. He hits for average and power. In slow-pitch he is a player who can easily hit a long fly ball for a sacrifice fly.

The number four hitter is the clean-up hitter. In slow-pitch, he is the big man who can hit the ball out of the park. The number-five hitter must be good enough to prevent the number-four hitter from being intentionally walked. He generally hits with power to all fields. The number six- through nine-hitters (and ten and eleven in slow-pitch) are the weaker hitters. These second-level hitters are not as critical in the batting order. They are listed in descending order of batting skill. Some teams put their weakest hitter in the next-to-the-last spot so that a decent hitter precedes the top of the order. You may want to put a streak hitter in the last spot so that, when he is hot, he'll be on base for the top of the order. If he is not hot, he is in the traditional spot for a weak hitter. One final consideration—never put a slow runner in front of a speedy one. Invariably the speedster lashes an extra base hit and has to slow down to avoid catching the slower lead runner.

Offensive Strategy (Slow-Pitch)

Since there is no stealing or bunting in slow-pitch softball, one of the most important offensive weapons is the ability to hit behind the runner, thus moving runners around with bat control. Coaches speak of making "productive outs" (outs that still help the offense by advancing runners). Many of the suggestions below work for fast-pitch, too.

If there are single runners on base (first, second, or third base only) with less than two outs, the batter must think about advancing the runner first, and getting a hit second. The hitter's job is to advance runners. If he can avoid making an out in the process, this is a bonus. With a runner at first only and less than two outs, the batter should hit the ball to the right side. There is less chance of the defense making a double play on a ball hit to the right side and more chance of a hit sending the runner all the way to third.

Other Situations and Hitting Strategy

If there is a runner on second and no outs, a ground ball to the right side or a fly ball to right-field will advance the runner to third. However, with one out, go for a hit because a runner on third with two outs is not a very advantageous situation for the offense.

If there is a runner on third and less than two outs, a ground ball or fly to the right side should drive in the run. A ground ball to the left side may result in the fielder holding the runner and throwing out the batter.

If the bases are loaded and there are no outs, hit the ball hard to right. A base hit scores two runs. A fly to right scores the runner from third and, with a tag up, moves the runner from second to third with still only one out. In the same situation, but with one out, it is not as beneficial to hit a fly to right, as tagging up will put the runner at third with two outs, making another hit necessary to score a run.

If there are runners at first and second, no outs or one out, hit to right again. Keep the ball away from the left side, where a fly ball tag-up is unlikely to be successful and a ground ball is likely to result in an easy out, with force-outs possible at second and third.

If there are runners at first and third, no outs or one out, a base hit to right scores one run and sends the runner from first to third. A ball hit to the left side could be an easy double play and, if it gets through to the outfield, the runner from first may hold at second.

If there are runners at second and third with no outs, hit to right again. A hit scores two runs, a ground ball scores one, and moves the runner from second to third with still only one out. With one out, still try to hit to the right side, but *any* deep fly will score the runner from third. With one out already, it is not as critical that the runner from second make third since his chances of scoring from third with two outs don't increase that much over his chances of scoring from second (there are no passed balls or wild pitches in slow-pitch softball).

As a general rule, always avoid easy fly balls. Try to hit the ball hard on the line or on the ground. Make productive outs, outs that advance runners or drive in runs.

Miscellaneous Offensive and Defensive Tips

The idea of strategy is to recognize and exploit the other team's weaknesses as well as recognize and counteract their strengths. For example, move your third baseman and first baseman in to take away the bunt from a team noted for its bunting ability.

If you have to, you can "hide" a weak-fielding player at the catching position in slow-pitch.

Practice everything that you are teaching. It doesn't do any good just to tell your baserunners that they are leaving too early on tag-ups. You have to hit fly balls to them in practice to let them tag up and experience leaving legally.

Check field conditions before each ball game. The ball skips off wet grass, bounces high off hard, dry ground, stops rolling quickly in deep grass. Pass this information on to your players.

Practice this: After hitting a line drive that's headed right at an infielder (an apparent easy out) have your batters *keep sprinting*. Often the fielder drops the ball, scrambles to recover it and, because the runner gave up on the hit, is able to throw him out at first.

Be daring when you are ahead or the score is tied. Also, play aggressively when there is no score early in the game. Play a more cautious game when you are behind. When planning strategy, always consider the importance of the run that a baserunner represents.

Attempt to score in every inning instead of playing for one or two big innings. Sell your players on the importance of getting the lead-off batter on base every inning.

When you are behind by a large margin, say 10-0 in the early innings, call the team together and remind them of how to play in this situation. The best strategy is to play for one or two runs, go to the field, put a zero on the scoreboard for the opponents, and then come in and get another run or two. Do this several innings in a row and you are right back in the game.

When you are behind by many runs and you get the bases loaded or runners on first and second, remind the runner at first that, on a base hit, you are likely to hold the runner from second at third. Because of the score, you are playing for a big inning and he should be prepared to hold at second on a hit that might ordinarily advance him to third. He must know this in advance or you might end up with two runners at third simultaneously.

In fast-pitch, with two outs, a runner on first, and a 3-2 count on the batter, the runner should take off for second as soon as the pitch is released. If the pitch is a ball, the batter walks and the runner can cruise into second. If the pitch is a strike, the batter is out and the inning is over. If the pitch is hit, the runner is already in motion toward the next base. With first and second bases occupied in the above situation, both runners should take off as soon as the pitch is released. With the bases loaded, however, the runner at third should walk, not run toward the plate as the batter may hit the ball down the third base line, creating a dangerous situation for the runner. The same procedure is used in slow-pitch, except that the runners leave their base when the ball reaches the plate.

In fast-pitch, when there is a runner on second or third, the second baseman or shortstop should back up every throw from the catcher to the pitcher. A wild throw would allow the runner to advance. Similarly, any time the first baseman throws the ball to the pitcher, the third baseman should back up the play. For example, with a runner at first the catcher attempts a pick-off. The runner is safe, and as the first baseman returns the ball to the pitcher, the baserunner may advance on an errant throw.

In the late innings of a close game, go with your best defensive players. Substitute your sure-fielding glove men into the line-up.

With the winning run at third and less than two outs in the last half of the last inning, play the outfield shallow enough to throw out a tagging runner. Playing shallow may allow them to catch a short fly or liner, and a longer fly will score the run anyway.

In slow-pitch, don't be afraid to change pitchers when the offense is hitting well. As in fast-pitch, the hitters sometimes catch on to your rhythm and get into a groove that a new pitcher might disrupt.

When the count is 3-0 and your hitter is letting the pitch go by, have him start to swing and then check it instead of squaring around and bobbing up and down to distract the pitcher. Umpires tend to call a very wide strike zone when the batter engages in these antics.

Scouting

Scouting is a way to catalogue a team's strengths and weaknesses. We feel that scouting is somewhat overrated in youth sports. The scouting report may say that a team is susceptible to a bunt offense, for example, but you still have to execute good bunts. Some teams try to do things they can't do well just because the scouting report calls for it. A team must always employ the tactics it does consistently well.

Scouting reports can tell you some very useful things, however. What type of pitch does the pitcher throw on the first pitch? What does he like to throw when ahead or behind in the count? What is his best pitch—(the one he'll probably throw in a crucial situation)? Does the pitcher tip off when he is going to throw a certain pitch? Does he rattle easily? Which batters hit the long ball and which are contact hitters? What pitches do they hit well? Are there any flaws in their stance, stride, or swing? In fast-pitch softball, does the catcher throw well? Does he have a quick release?

XII. Coaching a Youth League Team

Because youth sports have grown so large, with millions of youngsters participating, volunteer coaches are in great demand. In the forties, when Little League was in its infancy and the number of teams was much smaller, it was easy to find competent volunteer coaches. But today, most programs will take just about any coach who volunteers. Increasingly, parents are recruited to coach their own child's team, even if they have little or no sports background. We know of one parent who used to drop off his child at practice and stay to watch. When an additional team was formed, the league directors asked him to coach it, assuring him that he had "all the qualifications." Sure that he had no coaching expertise, he asked, "What qualifications do I have?"

"You're here!" was the curt, but very common answer.

So Ya Gotta Coach Your Kid's Team

There are usually two kinds of volunteer coaches today. One knows the sport (having played at the high-school level or beyond) and can communicate his knowledge to children, but wants to win at all costs. He treats his players well as long as they play well, but yells at or belittles them when they play poorly. He is the type who argues all the close calls with umpires and is just no fun to be around. The other type of coach is not a former athlete, doesn't know much about the game, but treats his players well and is a good role model. Many parents agree to coach their child's team to make sure that the team has an adult in charge who cares more about the kids than about winning. They figure that this is more important than knowing and teaching the game well—and they are right! With a little research, they can learn enough to do a good job. And it isn't necessary to be a former player to be a good coach. It is more important to be a *student* of the game. It is hard to find a coach who knows and can teach his sport *and* is the kind of human being you want in your child's life. The influence of a coach should not be underestimated. Many adults, when asked who the most important influences in their lives were, will list a former coach.

The ideal youth coach is one who can help his players become better athletes *and* better human beings. This is the ambitious goal that you should set for yourself if you accept a coaching position. Another important, and often overlooked, goal should be to make sure all of your players *have fun* playing softball. Youth sports have gotten so organized and so much under the control of adults that the sheer joy of playing often gets lost in the shuffle. A good argument can be made for league organizers just handing out the balls and bats and giving the kids access to the fields without any adult supervision. But, that isn't likely to happen in many areas. Your job, then, is to make your program have as positive an effect as possible on your players.

Before accepting a volunteer coaching position, be sure to "set a clear contract." Find out everything that will be expected of you. How many practices and games per week will you have? Is travel to games involved? If so, who will transport the children? What about liability insurance? Will you be asked to help at fund raisers? Will you have to pass out and/or collect uniforms, equipment, registration fees, raffle tickets? Will you be expected to umpire? Weigh the amount of time and effort you will put in against the benefits you expect to derive from coaching. Never agree in advance to coach a team for longer than one year. Also, consider the impact your coaching will have on your relationship with your child as well as his relationship with his teammates. You may have to discipline your child or his friends during the course of the season. Can you do this in a fair, objective, and consistent manner?

Once you decide to accept a coaching position, there is no turning back. If things do not go well during the season for whatever reason, you should *not* quit. Finish the season in as positive a fashion as possible, and tell the program director that you will be unable to coach again next season.

Player Selection

Youth leagues often have brief try-outs to select players for the various teams. Sometimes these are actual try-outs, in which some players will be "cut," and won't make a team. More often they are really player evaluations and every child will make one team or another. If 90 children register, the league might create 6 teams of 15 players each, or 7 teams, each with 12 or 13 players. The try-out is merely to evaluate the talent so that coaches can determine who they want to select in the up coming player selection meeting (known as "the draft").

During try-outs, each player wears a different number to identify him. When rating talent, the coaches are given a list of the players' names, numbers, and playing positions. Designated adults hit ground balls and fly balls to the players and pitch batting practice. Each player fields, throws, and hits while the coaches make note of each player's strengths and weaknesses. You can make up a rating system of your own, or you can write notes in the margins like "tall, lefty fielder, possible first baseman" or "good hitter and fielder, weak arm."

At most try-outs, organizers set up a station for timing the players in a sprint (40 or 60 yards, or just a home-to-first sprint). Never overlook speed when choosing players. A fast runner can help you on offense and defense.

If the try-out is well-organized, the different activities described will be going on in stations *simultaneously*. Therefore, it is best to have at least one helper when evaluating players.

Whenever we are involved with evaluations and player selection, we try to convince the other coaches to share information. We tell what we know about players and the other coaches do the same. It is better for everyone involved if the league is balanced than if one or two teams are loaded with good players.

We are amazed at how poor some volunteer coaches are at judging talent, which is, after all, one of the criteria for being a good coach. Before the draft, we rank order all the players (a computer helps) from the most to the least talented (in our judgment). This is very subjective and we use it only as a guide. When our turn to pick comes, we generally take the highest ranked player who is still available. We move players up and down on the list depending on our team's specific need (e.g., pitchers, catchers, etc.) but, in youth sports, a youngster's ability is more important than what position he has played in the past. A talented youngster can learn and adapt to new positions.

Your child will automatically be placed on your team unless you don't want him or he doesn't want you (options to consider). A common practice is to include the coach's child in the evaluation process. The other coaches rate him and make his parent select him on the appropriate round of the draft. If they deem that your child is one of the best players in the league, you must select him on the first round. If they decide that your child is a second-round player, you have to take him on your second pick. As you might expect, the other coaches always seem to rate your child a little better than he actually is.

If you know any of the local physical education teachers, it would be wise to pay them a visit before the draft. Bring your players' list with you and ask the teachers to clue you in about the youngsters. Find out about athletic ability *and* attitude. Pick a youngster who is going to be fun to work with over a top athlete who is a discipline problem. Coaching talented but rude and unappreciative athletes can make for a long, unpleasant season.

First Team Meeting

Once your players are selected, telephone each one, introduce yourself over the phone, and tell him the time and place of your first practice. Tell him what to wear (practice uniform, shorts, sweat suit), what to bring (glove, spikes, birth certificate, registration fee), and what time to have his parents pick him up after practice.

At the first practice, emphasize the importance of making a commitment to the team. Every player should try to attend every practice and game. Acceptable reasons for being absent include sickness and family commitments. Unacceptable excuses include "I had to go to the mall," or "We were having a yard sale." Supply each player with a team roster that lists everyone's telephone number (including yours and those of any assistant coaches). Inform them that they must call you as much *in advance* as possible if they will miss a practice or game. If they cannot reach you, they should call an assistant coach. Allow no surprise "no-shows" and no second-hand information such as "Coach, Sarah told me to tell you that she couldn't make it today." Explain that you need to know ahead of time who will miss practice because you will be making lesson plans like a schoolteacher. When a player you counted on is absent, it disrupts the lesson plan. The phone numbers also come in handy when a player wants to arrange for a ride with a teammate, or when he needs to confirm a schedule change.

Find out who on your team (or whose parent or sibling) is computer-savvy. Try to get that person to volunteer to help with typing (rosters, schedules, statistics, etc.). We especially like the computer programs that let you create your own monthly calendar. These can be used to print out the monthly schedule of games, practices, or tag days, and can be hung on the refrigerator for easy viewing. A player likes to have two of these—one for the "fridge" and one for his room. Once the children know the schedule of games and practices, tell the children there will be no changes unless you call them. For example, if it rains, they are to assume that the game is still *on* unless they hear from you. Again, no second-hand information as in "Frank told me the game was changed to Saturday."

This first meeting is the time to let the players know what they can expect from you, and what you expect from them. For example, tell them that there will be no throwing of bats and/or helmets after striking out. There will be no arguing with umpires (this goes for the coaches too—see below for instructions on how to diplomatically dispute a call). When rooting for the team during games, your players should say positive things about their own team rather than negative things about the opponents. They should say, "Come on Sue—you can hit this pitcher" rather than "This pitcher's awful, Sue, get a hit." Players should be expected to help carry equipment to and from the coach's car. Hint: After a couple of practices, you may find that some bats are never used. Take them out of the bat bag and store them in the garage or cellar. The less the equipment weighs, the easier it is to get someone to carry it.

One of the problems with coaching today stems from the fact that children start at such an early age and play on many different teams and in many different sports. They often have volunteer coaches who don't know the game, have little to teach them, and what they do teach is likely to be incorrect. Consequently, by the time the children get to you, they have pretty much learned *not to listen* when a coach is talking. We make it a point to tell our players that whenever we talk to them, *we have something to say*. We promise to keep our talks brief, and expect them to pay attention the entire time.

Team Meeting With Parents

The next order of business after the team meeting with the players is to set up a similar one with their parents. They should meet with you briefly before or after a practice. This meeting is for the parents and the coach to clearly understand what is expected of each other. First, make sure the parents understand that you are not being paid for coaching. Tell them that you responded to the league's request for non-paid help. You are looking for their cooperation. You may want to be candid about your level of expertise. If you want assistance from them, this is a good time to ask for it: assistant coach, scorekeeper, statistician, typist (how about newsletter editor?), help with fundraisers, someone to make telephone calls or to construct wooden gloves or batting tees.

Many parents register their youngsters for youth sports as a kind of babysitting service. If you have one game and one practice each week, that makes twice a week that parents can run errands, go shopping or see a movie without paying for a babysitter. Some will take advantage of you, if you let them. They will drop the youngsters off early, and pick them up late. Tell the parents that you will not keep them waiting. If you tell them practice ends at 8:00 P.M., end it at precisely that hour. Similarly, tell them you don't expect them to keep you waiting. When a practice or game ends, you expect the parents to be there to take their child home. (It is prudent on your part, however, to wait until you are sure that all your charges have their rides.)

Find out about any health problems that your players may have (child may be asthmatic, diabetic, allergic to bee stings, etc.). This is also the time to explain your philosophy of coaching. Explain what kind of commitment you expect from the children and how you intend to play them and make substitutions during games. Emphasize that adults can be deterrents to youngsters having fun, and you won't allow that to happen. Having fun and developing skills are more important than winning.

Be advised that no matter how good a coaching job you do, there are likely to be parents who are dissatisfied. Their child didn't play enough innings, you should have bunted at this time, you shouldn't have sent the runner home at that time, "You yelled at my baby!" Since you are a volunteer, and considering that those parents could very easily have coached the team instead of you, you have every right to expect parents not to be critical of your coaching. The majority of parents will be in your corner. Try to focus on that and disregard the whiners.

The Assistant Coach

Some coaches prefer working alone. Some like to have one assistant, others prefer two. It is better to coach alone than to team up with someone whose philosophy is radically different from yours. Problems will arise if one coach wants to keep the best players in for the entire game, and another wants to let everybody play an equal amount of time. Good relationships between coaches develop when they have complementary skills. For example, one might be the team's offensive coach and the other the defensive coach. You, the head coach, might be weak in one skill area, like pitching (or hitting), and therefore choose an assistant coach who is versed in that area.

We sometimes see teams with three coaches where one runs the practice and the other two sit around and chat. If you have assistants, utilize them and delegate responsibility. Find out their skills and put them to use. Keep your assistants informed. Have them over to your house for dinner, plan practices together, thank them for their help, give them credit at awards nights, say *we* instead of *I*, let them run the whole show (practice or game) once in a while, and never undermine the players' confidence in them by correcting them in front of the team.

Some Final Tips on Running Your Team

1. Be organized (see Chapter IX). Start and finish practice on time. Demand that players be on time and hustle always. Try to keep all players active during practice—no standing around. Use competition in drills to stimulate interest. Go from one drill to the next without wasting time. Remember that skills develop from repetition of drills augmented by coaches correcting mistakes. Don't introduce too many new concepts in one practice. Build up cumulatively and plan a good sequence of drills from one practice to the next. (Example: Go from Quick Tags with throws coming from one direction (left-field), to Quick Tags with throws coming from different directions, to Quick Tags and Bounce, to Quick Tags and Full-Arm Fake.) Try to use different drills to accomplish the same thing. Put new or difficult drills or techniques at the beginning of practice when players are more fresh and alert. Try to finish practice with something that is fun, something that leaves them eager to come back next practice. Have frequent, short practices rather than infrequent, long ones. If possible, follow an early-season practice with a movie, a cook-out, or a game against the parents.

2. Make your team a hustling unit. Get them sprinting to and from their fielding positions every inning. They must hustle whether or not they personally are having a good day or a bad one. Your goal is to win every game in hustle. Your team must never quit, no matter what the score. Youngsters need to learn how to compete well, more than how to win. Teach them to win and lose gracefully.

3. Be a fair and consistent disciplinarian. The penalty for being late or missing practice must be the same for every player, including your child. Tie in playing time to attendance, promptness, attitude, and work habits at practice. During games, encourage players on the bench to pay attention to the game. An assistant could be assigned to be the "bench coach" to teach the youngsters how to watch and learn from the play of others. The bench coach's job is a tough one, as attention spans are short in young children, and it seems against their nature to sit still, watch, and learn from the mistakes of others. The players, not coaches or umpires, should return bats and equipment to their proper place. They should stay in the dugout or team area and not wander off to sit in the bleachers with their parents or friends.

4. Correct your players' mistakes. Use a clipboard and pencil and write down errors (especially mental errors) and go over these before the next game.

5. Try to surround yourself with quality people. Don't just grab the first assistant who says he'll do it. If you have the luxury, be selective.

6. Communicate—make sure everybody knows what's happening (schedule for make-up games, upcoming fund raisers, etc.). A newsletter written by one of the players is perfect for this—and is not so ambitious a task thanks to today's revolution in "desktop publishing." Many home computers can help generate a nifty, inexpensive publication.

7. Take an objective look at your child and your relationship as coach to player. Treat him as close to the way you treat the other players as you can, while keeping in mind that it is impossible to treat him exactly like the others. You should give your child no more or less playing time than the others. On the other hand, another school of thought says, "I'm the volunteer coach. One of the benefits I get is playing my kid a few extra innings. If those other parents complain, why don't they coach?" Two schools of thought—it's your call, coach.

If you have to subjectively choose players for awards, selecting your own child as a recipient presents a sticky situation. Unless the child is a "hands-down favorite" for the award, we suggest you by-pass him.

8. Teach your team the philosophy: "Big Team, Little Me!" The success of the team is more important than the success of the individual. If you keep statistics (batting averages, etc.), don't let the players see them, as they promote concern for personal achievement. For the same reason, don't let them look through the scorebook.

9. Teach your players to leave the dugout or team area cleaner than it was when you arrived. Pick up your drinking cups and your gum or candy wrappers. Have each child pick up three of four other pieces of litter that were there when you arrived. Don't let any of the coaches chew tobacco or smoke while coaching.

What it Takes to Be a Good Coach

As we stated earlier, being an athlete or former athlete is not a prerequisite to becoming a good coach. Rather, a good coach must be a student of the game. He must be a motivator (a little charisma goes a long way), a communicator, a corrector of mistakes, a person who likes the sport and who likes kids. Good coaches are good judges of talent. They improve that talent and utilize it to their best advantage, and surround themselves with talented assistants.

The Final Word

How to Dispute an Umpire's Call (and not get thrown out in the process)

There is a genuine crisis in youth officiating, particularly in softball. The sport is growing so quickly that umpiring boards can't train new officials fast enough to keep pace. Local associations need so many umpires that it is difficult to maintain quality officiating. The larger the umpiring group, the tougher it is to insure quality. Take this as a given: There is likely to be poor officiating in your league. Moreover, the younger the age of the teams, the worse the officiating is likely to be. Youth leagues often become the training grounds for new umpires or the only place a board assignor will send a weak, veteran official. Some youth leagues use parents and coaches as "volunteer" umpires.

In any case, if an umpire makes a safe or out call with which you disagree, there is a tactful way to question the call and *possibly* get the decision reversed. First, make sure that no one else argues with the umpire but you, the head coach. Second, when time is called, go to the official who made the call and *calmly* talk with him. Try to convince him that perhaps he didn't get a good view of the play. Perhaps, for understandable reasons, of course, he was out of position (umpires often get themselves out of position while trying to elude batted balls or hustling infielders). Ask him, in the interest of fairness, if he would get a "second opinion" from the other umpire. If there is no doubt in his mind that he got the call correct, the umpire will not caucus with his "brother official." At this point you should go back to the team area and accept the call like a rational adult (no kicking equipment or players).

If he concedes that he may have missed the call (perhaps his view was screened by a player), he will probably go to his partner for help. If so, do not accompany him. Let the two officials talk it over. If the second official didn't see the play, or isn't any more sure of it than the first official, they will let the play stand as called. If, however, the second official is sure that the play was called incorrectly and tells his partner so, the umpire who made the call may reverse his decision. At this point, you say "Thank you for being fair to the children" and stand back to watch the other coach come flying out in a rage. In a short time you will see why umpires are reluctant to reverse their calls.

Note: If your league uses a one-umpire system, don't even bother registering your complaint about a missed call. The umpire has no "brother official" to confer with. Also, the critical factor in the success of the above strategy is the temperament of the coach when approaching the umpire. Umpires get very defensive, even obstinate, when harassed by rude, ill-mannered, soon-to-be ejected individuals. They are more likely to listen to your argument if they perceive you as an even-tempered, good-natured adult who is trying to rectify a mistake that was really no one's fault.

Appendix A. A Brief History of Softball

Since its beginnings over a hundred years ago, softball has grown faster than any other sport in the world. Many stories surround the actual origins of the game, some verifiable, some not, all fascinating. Through the years, softball has gone by many names: indoor baseball, playground ball, recreation baseball, kitten ball, ladies' baseball, soft baseball, mush ball, and sissy ball.

At the turn of the century, some professional baseball players felt that it would be beneficial to continue their play during the winter months. For most, playing outdoors was out of the question as was journeying south to join winter leagues. Thus, the idea of indoor baseball came about. Because indoor facilities (gyms and armories) were smaller than their outdoor counterparts, a large, soft ball was needed that would not travel as far as a baseball. With a few other rule and equipment changes, indoor baseball was ready to roll. Unfortunately for its developers and promoters, the idea never really caught fire. Some people attribute the lack of enthusiasm for indoor baseball to the players themselves, who found it impossible to psych themselves up for this new "recreation." No doubt the newly emerged concept of winter leagues in the Caribbean and South America and spring training in Florida and Arizona was far more appealing! Whatever the reason, indoor baseball soon went the way of the passenger pigeon, but the seed of softball had been planted.

Around this time, the names of George W. Hancock and Lewis Rober surfaced in connection with softball. Both men were from the Midwest, the birthplace and spawning ground of softball. Hancock, a member of the Farragut Boat Club of Chicago, is credited with developing softball as an indoor game in 1887. To restrict the ball's flight in the small indoor arenas, Hancock introduced a 16-inch softball with large raised seam ridges. This game flourished for several years, but, gradually became displaced by Lewis Rober's version of outdoor softball. A lieutenant in the Minneapolis fire department, Rober saw the sport as a means of keeping his firemen busy and in shape while they were on call at the firehouse. By 1895 Rober's outdoor game was the rage. He used a 12-inch softball that had a slick cover like a baseball, and the game he implemented was the precursor of modern softball. In quick succession, the first softball league ws established in Minneapolis in 1900 and the first rule book was written and published in 1906. Softball, which had begun as an indoor, poor-cousin version of baseball, was now out on its own fields and had begun its meteoric rise in popularity. It spread quickly, first throughout the Midwest, then the rest of the United States, and, finally, to Canada.

Organizations began to emerge, each trying to formalize and organize the game into a coherent, unified recreational activity. In 1908, the National Amateur Playground Association of Chicago published a rule book. When the National Recreation Congress met in 1923, at Springfield, Illinois, a splinter group called the Playground Baseball Committee was formed. Ten years later, this committee expanded into the Joint Rules Committee on Softball, which to this day governs the play of the game. In 1931 and 1933, the National Diamond Ball Association sponsored the first national softball tournaments in Minneapolis and Milwaukee respectively. Only a few states sent teams, however. A national cohesiveness was lacking, though struggling to emerge. The country was now in the throes of the Depression, a situation that, in fact, proved helpful to softball.

While the country suffered through the Great Depression, softball rode the crest of a wave of popularity that has continued to this day. Many thousands of people were out of work during this trying period and, as a result, had many hours of free time. Adults observed boys and girls involved in playground ball and became interested in the game. Taking to the many available playgrounds, they played this "child's game" passionately. With little or no work available, games were played primarily in the afternoon. When jobs once again became plentiful, the interest in softball did not wane, to the surprise of many. Instead of playing early afternoon games, workers now played after working hours and the concept of industrial "twilight softball" games was born. Leagues flourished wherever playgrounds were available throughout the United States and Canada.

About this time, two Chicagoans, Leo H. Fischer and M.J. Pauley, decided to utilize the city's numerous playgrounds by organizing local playground ball tournaments. These were so successful that Fischer and Pauley devised an ingenious plan: They would conduct a national championship at the Century of Progress World's Fair to be held in Chicago in 1933. After approaching the Fair officials and selling them on the idea, Fischer, who was sports editor of *The Chicago American,* and Pauley sent out promotional letters to twenty teams from different parts of the country, inviting them to take part in a tournament. This competition would decide the first national champion in *softball*, the name permanently affixed to this burgeoning sport by the two entrepreneurs. The name "softball" replaced "playground ball" because the game had now gone beyond the playgrounds of the country and was being played on thousands of vacant lots as well.

Because of softball's widespread popularity, Fischer's and Pauley's call was swiftly answered, and the teams soon assembled in the Windy City beneath the large towers of the Century of Progress, ready to play ball. The two men were shocked to find that each team played by its own set of rules, used different-sized bats and balls, and heeded no one governing body. It was then that Fischer formed the Amateur Softball Association and established the Joint Rules Committee. With uniformity and strong leadership, the way was set for softball to grow and expand at an almost limitless pace.

With the tremendous success of the national championship held at such a showcase as the Chicago World's Fair under their belts, Fischer and Pauley began promoting softball in a big way. The Amateur Softball Association (ASA) of America, with Fischer as its president, became the governing body of softball in the United States and eventually set up the International Softball Federation, which governs international play. Standardization has enabled softball to expand incredibly through the years, and the game is now one of the most popular international sports.

It is estimated that 40 million Americans, young and old, male and female, play softball (mostly slow-pitch softball). While one out of every six people play softball in the United States, the game is just beginning to take quantum leaps in foreign countries. Its growth has been projected at 10 to 15 percent each year—a truly amazing figure. In the last decade, the number of U.S. playing fields has risen from 75,000 to 120,000, but there is still a major shortage of playing space. This has led to private investors building outdoor and indoor softball complexes. One outdoor facility, for example, is built on 48 acres and has eight lighted playing fields, along with a playground, batting cages, a pro shop, patios, and a beer garden. Indoor softball is not as popular as the outdoor game, however, because of the smaller fields and different rules (e.g., shorter distances between bases).

Most communities are finding it difficult to keep pace with such phenomenal growth; internationally, the game is expanding, too. Softball's future looks bright indeed. Currently, it is included in the Asian and Pan American Games and there is talk that softball will even achieve Olympic Game status! The magnitude of this international acceptance has led to the prediction that softball will eventually supersede soccer as the world's most popular sport. This is quite a testimony for a game that had such humble beginnings.

Appendix B. Fund Raising for Your Team/League, Establishing a Team, Finding or Setting Up a Softball League

Fund Raising

Raising funds for your softball team or league can be a chore. Possibly a harder task than raising the money is finding someone to organize and oversee the fund-raising events. Raising funds can become a repugnant job when it is not done properly. Knowing *how* and *when* to raise funds in an organized way are two of the keys to success. The third is knowing what kind of event to hold. This appendix will assist you in your fund-raising endeavors, guiding you through the how, when, and what questions. First, let's discuss the responsibilities of whoever is in charge.

Your team or league is actually a small organization, comprised of the coaches, team members, parents, relatives, sponsors (if you have them), and friends. This is your core group; it is manageable, friendly, and willing to work. After all, you have a common goal: raising money for softball. As the coach, it should be your responsibility to do one of two things. You can put yourself in charge of the fund-raising activities and surround yourself with a reliable corps of volunteers, or you can delegate the leadership role to a responsible person from your core group and yourself become one of the reliable volunteers. Either way, your group needs a dependable leader who can take charge and deal firmly and fairly with the other members. Since you are a small group, the chairperson can easily divide the chores among the troops, and everyone can get about the business of raising money!

The person in charge selects the particular fund-raising event, develops the strategy, and coordinates the actual work to be done.

Meetings must be held to discuss all the fine points; coordination is the key to success. Once everyone knows his role and that he will be held accountable, the fund-raiser will go off smoothly. Never approach the fund-raiser in a slipshod way. Leaving details to chance and providing your volunteers with inadequate supervision is an invitation to failure or at best only limited success.

There are many ways to raise money for your organization, from direct solicitations and contributions to fun-filled, entertaining events in which the entire community can participate. The fund-raiser can be a one-shot deal, or an annual occasion that everyone looks forward to. So, choose your event and have fun!

Old Stand-bys

1. Bake sales: All members donate food and time to the sale. Choosing the site where it will be held is important. Don't be afraid to hold the sale in several locations on the same day. If your town or local area has several stores in a grocery chain, contact the store managers and get permission to hold the sale in each store on the same day. It takes some planning, but it can be done. Expand your sale beyond dessert items to include casseroles, pasta dishes, homemade breads, jams, jellies, relishes, and so on. For the industrious crew, put together and sell a cookbook of the group's favorite recipes.

2. Car washes: Clean both interior and exterior!

3. Candy sales: This is a good fund raiser if you can find a wholesaler who is willing to divide the sales 50/50. Stick with known brands rather than exotic, unfamiliar ones.

4. Magazine subscriptions: If organized correctly and done with the proper wholesaler, this can be a *huge* money raiser. Be sure you are offering well-known magazines that appeal to the majority of people. This can be an annual event because people are likely to want to renew their subscriptions. To insure satisfaction, be sure to provide customers with toll-free numbers for the wholesaler/distributor in case there are problems with magazine delivery. You should also be willing to assist people with any complaints.

5. Gift wrapping paper: Again, with the right supplier (one willing to split the profits 50/50 or 60/40), this can be a big fund raiser. Try to sell high-quality paper that has a broad appeal, such as a combination of Christmas, birthday, and all-purpose wrap in varying patterns and avoid gift wrap that is suitable for only one occasion.

6. Candles/greeting cards: Quality and variety are important here. When quality is sacrificed for price, people will be less eager to buy when you knock once again on their doors. If possible, offer samples from a varying price range.

7. *Light bulbs:* These are universally needed, and always in an assortment of sizes.

8. *Pot holders/jar openers:* Stock useful items that may be sold throughout the softball season (on a table set up at your games). Include on this table the light bulbs from above, candy, cushions with team or league logo (great for those cold, hard, wet bleachers).

9. *Tag days:* This is group begging day, when team members invade shopping malls, banks, gas stations, and intersections with red lights, holding out containers for contributions. This does not improve the self-image, but it can be a productive fund-raiser if *all* help to collect. Hint: It is difficult for people to ignore *children* whose softball season seems to be in jeopardy.

10. *Yard/garage sales:* Have the entire team clean out the garages, attics, and cellars of their houses and find a big yard to hold the sale in. It might be worthwhile for your group to rent space (usually fairly inexpensive) at a local flea market. This way you are assured of a steady stream of customers who have spending in mind. It also helps to advertise your yard sale in the newspaper, on the radio, or on the community access channel of the local cable television company.

11. *Thons:* Another successful fund raiser for sports is the "thon." Jogathons, walkathons, and swimathons are very popular today. The athletes get sponsors (parents, relatives, friends, etc.) to pledge a certain amount of money per lap swum, mile walked or run, etc. Softball players might garner pledges for each inning that they participate in a *marathon* softball game. If a sponsor pledges 10¢ per inning and the player makes twenty innings, that is a $2.00 profit. If he gets fifteen sponsors, that will make $30.00 for his effort. If each of fifteen players on your team does likewise, the team collects $450.00. An eight-team league could clear $3000 on one long day of softball. (Play a 100-inning game on a week-end. Rotate players in and out of the line-up and serve refreshments. Give each player a target to shoot for in total pledges and set a limit on the total that can be collected from one sponsor. Keep in mind that collecting from sponsors rarely results in a 100% return.)

For the More Ambitious

1. *Direct solicitation:* Your team/league can go directly to the businesses in the community and ask for money. When using this approach, stress the importance of the team/league and the community

service that it performs. Each team may have a sponsor (small business to corporate giant) who provides money for necessary items; but don't overlook other businesses that are not sponsors but may wish to contribute in order to improve their public image. Direct solicitation may also involve canvassing the neighborhoods, asking everyone to fund the fine work being done for your town's youth. Make this fund-raiser a yearly event, and, above all, make every effort to publicly recognize the contributors (large or small).

2. *Fence advertising:* If the league's playing fields are enclosed by fencing, sell the space on the fence to local businesses for advertising. The best way to do this is to contract someone to cut and paint plywood signs (or do it yourself). These can be attached to chain-link fences quite easily and can be repainted or replaced with signs for a new advertiser in the future. This gimmick works well because it is relatively inexpensive (an average of $100 for the first year, $50 per year for renewals) and provides daily advertising to large groups of people. When selling the space, stress to the potential renter that people seeing the advertisement will appreciate the fact that his business supports the youth league.

3. *Pot-luck supper:* This is a fairly inexpensive and effective fund-raiser to hold, and it has the added bonus of providing a pleasant atmosphere for people to gather. First, find a hall (church and school halls are sometimes free) that has tables, chairs, refrigerators, and stoves/ovens. Team/league members prepare a dish (usually a casserole) that will serve 10 or more people and bring it to the supper. Obviously, the food should be plentiful and delicious! Charge an admission price: $2 to $3 for adults and $1 for children and senior citizens, who love this type of event. Members who do not cook a dish can pay double to get in, or they can pay the regular admission and clean up afterward. Non-cooks can also bring cheese, fruit, desserts, etc. Don't forget to set up your gift table, offering recipe books, candy, light bulbs, potholders, and other items.

4. *Raffles:* Everybody loves a raffle! They're easy to run, the profit is good, and the repeatability is very high (some organizations hold monthly raffles). The usual price of $1 a ticket or $5 for six tickets enables people of all ages and from every income bracket to participate. People love the thrill of possibly winning big prizes for a low initial investment. These two factors (small price, big prize) make it easier for everyone to sell the tickets, from child to senior citizen, and the tickets can be whipped out almost anywhere the seller sees a chance to make a quick sale. Some things to remember before you

start selling tickets. First, check with the local and state governments to determine if a license is needed to hold a raffle. Next, print the tickets. Mimeographing your own tickets obviously saves money but, if your budget allows, you may opt to have them professionally printed. We recommend that you print your own. On each ticket, be sure that you list the date and location of the drawing, prizes, price, and a number. Each ticket should have a detachable stub where the buyer writes his name, address, and telephone number.

Selecting the type of prizes is also important. Try to get local merchants to donate prizes because the more you spend on prizes, the lower your profit margin. Just about anything is suitable for prizes: shopping sprees, liquor, free maid service, vacations, automobiles, art lessons, hair styling, bowling lessons—be creative! Suit your prize list to your community. Probably the most popular prize is cash; sometimes, the winner will donate a portion of his winnings back to the organization.

The coordinator of the raffle must keep track of who has how many tickets, collect money and ticket stubs at designated times, and is responsible for seeing that members have an ample supply of tickets to sell. Giving a prize to the top 3 ticket sellers is a good incentive; so is rewarding the person who sells the winning ticket.

5. Dance: More ambitious than the pot-luck supper, a dance also requires a little more preparation. First, rent a room or a hall, book a band or disc jockey (well in advance), choose a theme (if desired), and advertise well. Select a band or D.J. carefully. You want one that is not only good, but that plays the type of music you want. A good, popular band or D.J. makes selling tickets easy. Remember: If people enjoy the music and have a great time, it will be much easier to sell tickets for next year's dance!

The hall must have ample space to dance, sit, and buy beverages. Keep the alcoholic drinks simple (nothing exotic that's difficult to mix) and offer beer, wine, and soft drinks for sale. Selling separate tickets at the door for drinks may be a good idea: one ticket (50 cents) for soft drinks, two tickets ($1) for beer and wine, three tickets ($1.50) for mixed drinks. (with this method, any unused tickets are all profit!) Provide coffee, and non-alcoholic fruit punch, and snacks (popcorn, peanuts, pretzels) free. If you feel really ambitious, sell sandwiches and pizza too.

For added fun, give the dance a theme: Choose from seasonal themes, costume balls (Halloween), Mardi Gras, toga, Roaring Twenties, Fifties, oldies-but-goodies—the list is limitless! Take advantage of your captive audience to sell the usual items or hold the drawing for your raffle.

6. *Las Vegas nights:* Check with local government about getting a permit to run these gambling galas. (Some areas allow youth or community groups to run several of these per year.) Book a hall and a gaming contractor (well in advance). The contractor provides gaming tables, cards, poker chips, and assistance on the night of your event. You must provide workers (dealers for blackjack or poker, people to operate the roulette wheels, and so on). Most contractors will run a "clinic" before the gambling starts to teach your workers how to operate their tables. At the end of the night (Vegas nights generally run from 7:00 or 8:00 P.M. to midnight), tally your receipts. The contractor takes either a flat fee or a percentage of the receipts. A friendly contractor (who wants your return business) will take a smaller "cut" if he sees that your group has not had a good night financially.

7. *Auctions:* For an auction, all items are donated, so the profit margin is terrific. Buying items to auction puts a lot of pressure on you (or the auctioneer) to make a profit; try to avoid this kind of aggravation. Once again, the goods to be auctioned can be varied, from the commonplace to the off-beat (maybe even downright bizarre): artwork, jewelry, tickets to the theater, rock concerts, sporting events, trips, cars, restaurant meals, golf lessons, aerial balloon rides, skydiving lessons. Contact local merchants for goods, neighbors for services (resumes typed, cars washed and waxed), and members for their help. Advertising is crucial for an auction, as is hiring a professional auctioneer. Unless you *know* that one of your members can pull this off, go for the pro. Sell tickets for the auction and be sure that each ticketholder receives a copy of the program in advance. They have bought and deserve the advantage of planning their bidding strategy ahead of the others. If possible, allow these people to mail in bids if they are not going to be present; keep the bids sealed until that item is offered for auction. The program should be attractively prepared and meticulously accurate. Organization members can collect tickets, assist the auctioneer, and sell refreshments. Keep the atmosphere lively and up-beat; excited, happy people are apt to spend more money.

8. *Cinema/theater parties:* These are fun events and easy to run. Contact a local cinema or playhouse and inquire about purchasing a large block of tickets (or, better yet, the entire house). You should receive a discount rate (40 to 50 percent or more) for buying so many tickets; then, simply resell the tickets for a higher price. Choose a movie or play that appeals to the majority of your people; stay away from avant-garde productions.

9. *Haunted House:* Run this proven successful fund-raiser during Halloween. Select an older home or building with a spooky exterior, or a gym or hall or any place whose interior can be made to look scary. Collect an admission fee at the entrance. The customers walk through, one way, are frightened along the way and exit at the opposite end. The more ghoulish sights and sounds (ghosts, banshees, Dracula) you include along the trip, the better. Make the area dark enough to be scary, but light enough to insure safety (you may want to inquire about liability insurance). The word about a really grisly haunted house spreads quickly and you will find children returning with their friends. With imagination, other holidays can provide similar events.

10. *Cow chip contest:* This is one of the most unusual fund-raisers that we know of. It is best done as an attraction at a fair or bazaar. The idea is to section off a large field (football and soccer fields work well) into small squares. Use lime for this. Sections can be as small as 1 square foot. For example, a regulation football field can provide 5000 squares. The squares are numbered and tickets with corresponding numbers are sold for, say, $10 each. On the day of the event, a well-fed cow is released onto the field, allowed to graze and roam, and eventually drops a chip. The lucky owner of the square into which the first chip falls wins the prize. A substantial prize, say $5000, is recommended. This is a simple way to turn nearly $45,000 in profit—no bull.

Establishing a Team

Locating Players

Finding players for your softball team is not as difficult as it may seem; there are many athletes and potential stars waiting for the call to action. The trick lies in knowing where to locate them and how to get them to sign up for the team.

1. Start with your own children, as players or recruiters. Your kids will know plenty of others who want to play. Word spreads quickly about a new team.

2. Post notices on the school, recreation center, and church bulletin boards. Put information in the school newspaper and church bulletin. Go to the schools and ask each principal to announce the formation of a team. Supply flyers and sign-up sheets.

3. Visit your local schools' softball teams' practices and games. Meet each coach and tell him about your proposed team. Stress to him that you would welcome his players into your progam.

4. Have the local newspaper report your team's formation in the sports section. Use the local radio's public service announcements and cable television's community access channel to advertise.

Once the team has been formed, the next order of business is to locate practice and playing fields. (If fields are scarce or heavily used in your area, you may want to consider this step *before* establishing a team.)

1. Check with the recreation department in the town hall about the availability of fields. Usually, you will need a permit to use them.

2. Contact the school recreation department, churches, civic centers, and private industry about the availability of their fields. Often, these places are more than willing to help out with local youth programs.

Finding or Setting Up a Softball League

Finding a suitable league is next on the agenda. There is probably already a league that will accept your team as long as you have a sponsor, a roster, and the cash for the entry fee. Approach the recreation department, churches, and civic centers for possible entry into leagues, and check the sports page for the formation of new leagues or the expansion of existing ones. If, after all this, you cannot find or get into a suitable league, consider establishing your own. It's not difficult, and being the commissioner has its rewards.

1. Advertise the formation of your league in the usual spots: radio, television, newspaper, bulletin boards.

2. Accept the applications of prospective teams (four teams should be the minimum). Be sure that each has a sponsor. Get payment up front for operating fees. These include umpires, equipment, and insurance.

3. Assemble new coaches or team representatives for initial meeting, of which you will be chairman. Accept nominations for and elect league officers: president, vice-president, and secretary/treasurer.

4. Write a charter, outlining your by-laws. Include the following:

    A. Purpose of organization

    B. Length of term for officers

    C. Duties of officers

D. Elections (when held, nominating procedure, secret ballot or voice vote, etc.)

E. Recall provision

F. Quorum rules (e.g., a third of registered members)

G. Voting rules (simple majority or quorum is best)

H. Dues (if any)

I. Meetings (where, when, and how ofter)

Once the hierarchy of the group has been determined, turn your attention to your league operating rules. Give some hard thought to these since they will govern the style and caliber of play in the league. Here are some suggestions:

1. Collect team rosters before the first game.

2. Schedule games and distribute copies to all.

3. Establish starting game times, with forfeiture time included (usually 15 minutes after game time).

4. Determine rules for uniforms: do you want team shirts with numbers, shirts and pants, hats, etc.?

5. Decide rules to abide by: e.g., Amateur Softball Association (A.S.A.) or United States Slo-Pitch Softball Association (USSSA) and make sure all coaches have the correct, current rule book.

6. Amend the rules to suit your league's purposes. For example, your league may want free substitution, unlimited pitching arc (slow-pitch softball), courtesy runner, etc.

7. Choose the kind of softballs to be used (particular brand name, restricted flight, etc.) and who will supply them (home team, both teams, the league).

8. Establish procedures for postponements and rescheduled games.

9. Determine the rules governing players deemed ineligible because of age, suspensions, etc.

10. Write ground rules for each field used and make sure all coaches and umpires have a copy.

If possible, you or one of your league officers should have access to a computer. The paperwork will be less difficult and time-consuming.

Your league should contract with a local umpiring board to secure bona fide officials for your games. We recommend that you do not try to save money by opting for volunteer umpires. All you will get for this is free trouble! Do not jeopardize your league's integrity. Hire people who know the rules and have no vested interest in your games. The coaches and, most of all, the players will be grateful for that decision. Sit down with the president of the local umpires' board and work out an agreement that stipulates fees, number of umpires per game, duration of contract, and so on. Having those men in blue will give stability and credence to your league.

Ensuring communication among the members (players, coaches, parents) of your league is important. Talk over problems with each other; keep the lines of communication open. A good approach is to write a brief newsletter relaying the league's news to everyone concerned. (Here, again, a computer will come in handy.) The newsletter can contain softball anecdotes, scores, game highlights, problems encountered during games and their resolutions, upcoming events (tournament news, fund-raisers, awards nights, etc.), and coaching pointers.

Appendix C. Equipment

The Necessities

Bases (tie-down)	$30–50 set of 3
Bat bag	$15–55
Bats (aluminum, 26-31 in.)	$16–40
Bats (aluminum, 33-36 in.)	$21–100
Catcher's gear:	
Mask and helmet	$20–30
Throat protector	$3–5
Chest protector	$20–30
Leg guards	$20–30 pair
Helmets	$13–25 each
Scorebook	$5–20
Softballs	$36–50 dozen
Uniforms, includes:	
Shirt (with team name	
and number)	
Hat	
Stirrups (socks)	
Pants	
Total per uniform	$17–60

The Extras

Ball bag	$15–25
Bases (rubber, throw-down, good for baserunning drills indoors or outdoors)	$12–15 (set of 3 bases, home plate, pitching rubber)
Bases (Hollywood type, immovable, fit into ground receptacle)	$150–250 set of 3
Bases (break-away)	$300 set of 3
Bat (A.S.A. warm-up)	$35
Batting tee	$15–25
Cones (practice)	$2–4 each
Fungo bat (aluminum)	$35
(wood)	$16
Pitching machine	$1,000
Rag balls	$30–45 dozen

Appendix D. SOFTBALL AND SAFETY

Softball safety must be of prime concern to coaches and players. Softball injuries are going to happen, but certain steps can be taken to reduce their frequency. Carelessness, inadequate coaching instruction (particularly sliding technique), sub-standard equipment, lack of physical conditioning, and alcohol consumption (in adult softball leagues) are the major contributors to softball injuries. As a coach, you must take steps to better insure the safety of your players.

Players can take steps to insure their own safety, too, especially in their choice of equipment. They should purchase the highest quality equipment they can afford. Coaches should insist that each team member wears athletic shoes with cleats, either metal, rubber, or hard plastic. (Before buying metal cleats, check to see if your league rules or affiliation allows them.) Sneakers should never be worn for softball because they provide insufficient traction, and their use can lead to serious injuries. This is particularly true on muddy fields and wet grass. Sliding pants/pads can help prevent contusions and abrasions, the result of hard baserunning and sliding.

Approved batting helmets with protective earflaps on both sides are a must, whether at bat or on the basepaths. In some leagues, a player is out if he intentionally removes his helmet while batting or running the bases. For safety reasons, and to get your players accustomed to the headgear, make them wear helmets in practice during baserunning and hitting drills.

A catcher's helmet or skull cap is recommended for your catcher. He also needs a mask with a throat guard, a chest protector, shin guards, and, for males, a protective cup and supporter to shield the groin. We recommend that even your slow pitch catchers wear full gear because thrown bats are a major hazard in games. Make any player who warms up the pitcher wear a catcher's mask, no matter how slowly the pitcher throws. We often see maskless catchers in fast pitch, warming up pitchers between innings. A pitch in the dirt could bounce up and cause injury. Even worse, some catchers place the mask in front of them, on or near home plate, inviting disaster.

Get your catchers used to wearing full gear in games *and* in practice. Make them wear it for infield practice and when practicing throwing out stealing baserunners. In games they'll have to throw encumbered by the gear, so they should get used to how it feels to make the plays in practice. It is also a good idea to teach your catchers to keep the mask on if making a play at the plate. Too many toss the mask aside, preferring not to peer through it while awaiting a throw. Since catchers can see through the mask well enough to catch seven innings worth of fastballs, they should be able to see well enough to catch a ball and tag a sliding runner. Besides, you want your catcher to have full protective gear in case of a collision with a speedy baserunner.

Mouth guards are excellent for protecting players' teeth and are strongly recommended by orthodontists. Make sure your players who wear eyeglasses use a safety strap, and doctors highly recommend safety glass lenses.

Encourage all players in the field to wear baseball caps; besides looking sharp, the caps will shield their eyes from the sun and keep their hair from obstructing their vision. The team's softball gloves and mitts should be top quality, well-cared for, and frequently inspected for loose ties or ripped webbing. During practice sessions and games, exposed jewelry (necklaces, earrings, watches, bracelets, etc.) should not be worn because it can become entangled, and injury may result. The Amateur Softball Association allows participating players to wear medical alert bracelets and necklaces as long as they are taped securely to the body. Players should not be allowed to play or practice with plaster casts, but braces, if covered by soft material, are allowed. However, try to keep an injured player out of the line-up, even if he's the star and this is "the big game." If in doubt, secure a medical release before playing him. As coach, you are entrusted to put the welfare of the player ahead of the outcome of the game.

Field awareness is another vital part of softball safety. For example, before a game, the coaches and players should inspect the field for idiosyncracies: holes or dips in the ground, sharp objects (remove glass, metal, and large stones), unsafe fence sections, proximity of trees and other bordering objects. Inspecting and becoming familiar with the field can prevent injury by alerting players to potential dangers.

There are many avoidable collisions in softball. Fielders run into each other while chasing batted balls; baserunners smack into fielders as they round the bases. Coaches must drill fielders to communicate on defense (see Chapter IX). Also, coaches must teach their infielders to move *inside the diamond* when a baserunner is rounding their bag. For example, when the batter hits a drive for extra bases, the first baseman should move inside the diamond as the baserunner's momentum will take him outside. The umpire would rule a collision obstruction by the fielder. By moving inside, he avoids obstruction and can make sure the runner touches the base (or appeal the runner missing the bag).

During games or practices, a player should be "heads-up" at all times, whether participating or not. Every player, on the bench or in the field, should always know where the ball is. We have seen players, strolling across the field during batting practice, get struck by a line drive. As described in Chapter III, instruct your players never to throw the ball to a teammate unless he indicates his readiness to accept the throw by giving a proper target.

Keep all equipment in one section of the bench area, away from players entering and leaving. Batters, warming up in the on-deck circle, should make sure that all bats are returned to the bench. Also, while on deck, they should only swing one or two bats or an approved warm-up bat. Because they are dangerous, never allow players to swing homemade weighted bats, lead pipes (slippery), or bats with bat rings attached. In addition, if the safety grip comes off the bat, replace it or tape the bat handle using friction tape. A well-organized practice is a safe practice (see Chapter IX). Using common sense is the key to reducing injuries while on the softball diamond.

Proper year-round conditioning helps keep your players injury-free, too (see Chapter I). Be sure your players stretch, run, and warm up their arms properly before practices and games. Correct throwing technique helps prevent arm injuries (see Chapter III).

It is important to stress to the team that their ability to stay off the disabled list is contingent upon their overall fitness. Strong, well-conditioned, flexible bodies tend to stay injury free, and when hurt, the fit athlete has a faster recovery time than the unfit one. Mental alertness, as well as physical fitness, keeps the good softball player "up" and aware, ready to avoid that potential season-ending injury.

According to a study reported in the Journal of the American Medical Association (JAMA), 71% of recreational softball injuries over a four-year period were due to base sliding. Many of these injuries resulted from the impact of fast-moving players with stationary bases. From this study, a team of medical and recreation experts set up another study to compare breakaway bases with stationary ones. Over 600 games were played on fields with breakaway bases and the same number were played on diamonds with stationary bases. The players were aged 18 to 55 and represented a wide range of skill and experience levels. There were 45 sliding injuries on the fields with stationary bases (about 1 injury every 14 games) and only two on the breakaway base fields (about 1 injury every 316 games). Most injuries involved the slider's lead foot or hand.

We recommend using breakaway bases in conjunction with teaching proper sliding technique. These bases are expensive, and their cost may be prohibitive; they cost about twice as much as stationary bases. Teaching proper sliding mechanics, however, can be done with little or no cost (see Chapter VI).

Finally, we highly recommend that you have a well-stocked first aid kit on hand for games and practices. If you have a trainer available to your program, take advantage of this luxury. Be sure that each member of your team has his own medical insurance or is enrolled in the league's group plan.

Appendix E. Scoring

Keeping score of a softball game is more than just tallying runs and hits; it is an accurate pitch-by-pitch, play-by-play, inning-by-inning account of the action. The competent scorer, besides being versed in the rules of softball, must have a working knowledge of scorer's shorthand, a seemingly cryptic writing that, when deciphered, tells the entire story of a game.

The main concern of the scorer is keeping track of the score and the inning; in the end, all anyone cares about is who won and how many hits he got, right? Wrong! There are many other concerns as well: strikeouts, walks, errors, to name a few. The complete scorer maintains a complete scorebook, and becoming familiar with some of the basics is essential. First, the conscientious scorer arrives 20 to 30 minutes before game time, armed with his scorebook, which already contains the teams' names, the date, and the name of the field. Next, the umpires' names are added and, when available, the line-ups are penciled in, with the players' names and uniform numbers entered in the proper order. The names and numbers of all substitute players should be added now, to expedite matters if and when they enter the game. Next to the players' names, the scorer should also indicate, by number, their field positions, These are:

Position	Number
Pitcher	1
Catcher	2
First baseman	3
Second baseman	4
Third baseman	5
Shortstop	6
Left fielder	7
Center fielder	8
Right fielder	9
Short fielder (slow-pitch)	10

These numbers not only assist player indentification, but they also are invaluable when recording the play in the scorebook. For example, when recording a fly out to the center fielder, the scorer simply marks F-8, F signifying a fly out and 8 indicating the center fielder. Similarly, a ground ball out, from the shortstop to the first baseman, is recorded in the scorebook as 6-3.

The idea of using standardized symbols is to enable anyone to re-create the events of a game simply by deciphering the code. On the other hand, a scorer often develops his own "language" that explains the simplest to the most complex play. This is acceptable and often unavoidable. Following are some of the common symbols used by official scorers:

Play	Symbol
Assist	A
Base on balls (walk)	BB
Caught stealing (fast-pitch)	CS
Double	2B
Double play	DP
Error (fielding)	E
Error (throwing)	ETh
Fielder's choice	FC
Flyout	F
Hit by pitch (fast-pitch)	HBP
Home run	HR
Infield fly	IF
Intentional walk	IBB
Passed ball (fast-pitch)	PB
Putout	PO
Sacrifice fly	SF
Single	1B
Stolen base (fast-pitch)	SB
Strikeout (called)	KC
Strikeout (swinging)	K
Triple	3B
Wild pitch (fast-pitch)	WP

The typical scorebook has boxes opposite each player's name, inside which the scorer records the result of each at-bat. The box usually contains a small softball diamond. More elaborate score-books contain spaces to keep track of the ball-strike count, an out box, and an RBI box. Even more elaborate books contain some of the common symbols noted above, which can be checked off to facilitate matters. Illustrated below are three examples of an individual scoring box:

The economy version: *The intermediate version:*

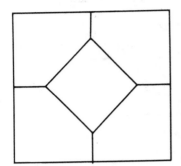   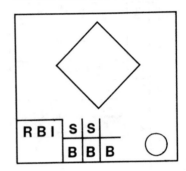

The deluxe version:

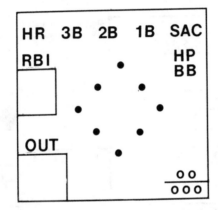

Using the intermediate scorebook version, we have simulated two innings of softball. (See sample on page 230.)

After working the count to two balls and one strike, Rowe, the first batter of the inning, grounds out to the second baseman. The scorer indicates this by darkening the ball/strike indicator, writing 4-3 in the diamond, and inserting a 1 in the out box. The next batter, Cash, lines an 0-2 pitch to right field for a single. The scorer shows the flight of the ball from home plate (on the small diamond) to right field and then tracks the path of the batter by drawing a line from home plate to first base. The symbol 1B is written in the box. If using the deluxe version of the scorebook, the scorer would simply check off 1B. Stevens, the third batter of the inning, takes a called third strike, and a KC is placed in his box, followed by a 2 in the out box. Tyler flies out to center field, ending the inning. The scorer puts F-8 in the box and a 3 in the out box. Notice that a diagonal line under Tyler's name

No.	LINE UP	POS	1	2	3
6	1 ROWE	9	4-3 (1)	4-6-3 / 6-3 OP 3	
14	2 CASH	2	1B		
20	3 STEVENS	3	KC (2)		
31	4 TYLER	6	F-8 (3)		
1	5 JOHNSON	4		E-6 BB	
3	6 FITCH	5		E-6	
5	7 SANDERS	7		HR 3	
22	8 CRAFT	1		1-3 (1)	
15	9 BENSON	8		4-6 / BB 2	
	10				

TOTALS		RUNS	0	3	
		H	E	LOB	
		1	0	1	1	1	0

ON THE BENCH	
2	DAVIS
33	BAILEY

indicates that he was the final batter in the inning. Finally, the scorer totals the runs and hits for the inning and places these numbers in the appropriate spots at the bottom of the scorebook.

In the next inning, Johnson leads off by drawing a walk on a 3-1 pitch. Fitch hits the first pitch to the shortstop, who bobbles the ball for an error. Everybody's safe! Note how Johnson's advancement to second base has been scored. On a 2-2 count, Sanders hits a three-run homer and gets credit for three runs batted in. The scorer must show that all three players have scored by darkening each diamond. Craft grounds out to the pitcher, and Benson walks on four straight pitches. Rowe ends the inning by grounding into a 4-6-3 (second-short-first) double play. Notice that Benson's out reads 4-6 and Rowe, who hit into the 4-6-3 double-play, is out on the 6-3 end of the twin killing.

A competent scorer makes the game flow smoothly by doing his job accurately. A coach enjoys the luxury of having a reliable scorekeeper on the bench, and, of course, the players love seeing a precise record of their accomplishments. (Warning: A scorer's decisions may not endear him to every player.)

Appendix F. Amateur Softball Association (A.S.A.) Softball Rules in Consumer English

Appeal play: The umpire cannot call this play until a member (manager, coach, or player) of the offended team asks him to. The most common appeal plays occur when a runner misses a base or leaves a base too early on a tag-up (when tagging up to advance after a fly-ball catch, a runner may leave his base when the ball is first touched by the fielder). Let's say a runner misses second base while running from first to third. The umpire sees it, but must wait until the play is over and someone on defense says, "Hey, ump. He missed second." Now the umpire can call him out. There is no need to tag the runner or the base missed. Just say clearly which runner you are appealing and what infraction you feel occurred. All appeals must be made before the next pitch (legal or illegal) and before your pitcher and infielders leave fair territory. Well-coached infielders watch runners step on (or miss) their base and know how to execute a proper appeal.

Catch: If the ball is held in your hand, glove, or both, it is a legal catch. It is no catch if the ball is merely held against the body with the arms. If the fielder catches the ball, then immediately collides with a teammate, a wall, or the ground, and drops it, it is not a catch. If the fielder drops the ball while beginning to throw it, umpires generally rule that the fielder has completed the play of catching the ball, and is starting a new play, that of throwing it. The out stands.

Charged conference: On defense, a charged conference occurs when the coach calls time out and goes onto the field to talk to the pitcher. After the second charged conference in the same inning, the pitcher must be removed from the pitching position. He can pitch no more that game, but he *can* play another position. On offense, a charged conference occurs when the coach calls time and talks to the batter or baserunner. Only one offensive charged conference per inning is allowed.

Dislodged base: This is a base that was moved from its proper place (usually by a baserunner). Play can continue, with runners tagging the approximate spot where the base was before it was dislodged. If a runner remains in the area of a dislodged base, he cannot be tagged out. However, if he wanders off toward the next base, the umpire may rule that he is in jeopardy of being tagged out. When the play ends, the base is put back where it belongs.

Dropped third strike: Fast-pitch: If the catcher does not catch the third strike *and* there are less than two outs *and* first base is unoccupied, the batter may attempt to advance to first base. If he gets there before the catcher retrieves the ball and throws it to the first baseman (who catches it and touches the bag), he is safe. If first base is occupied, the batter is out and cannot advance. However, any time there are two outs when a dropped third strike occurs, the batter *can* run to first base (even if it is already occupied). In all the instances above, other baserunners may advance, as the ball is considered live.

Notes about dropped third strikes: If the batter may not advance but the runner at first base does, any play on him is a tag play. However, with bases loaded and two outs, for example, a play on any runner is a force out (they are forced to run by virtue of the batter becoming a baserunner). Finally, with two strikes in fast-pitch softball, a pitch that short hops to the catcher is considered a dropped third strike. Teach your catchers to tag the batter, if possible, rather than throw to first.

Slow-pitch: The batter is always out on a dropped third strike, but A.S.A. has another third strike rule for slow-pitch games. The batter is out if, with two strikes on him, he hits a foul ball. If the foul ball is caught by any fielder, the ball is live and runners may tag up and advance at their own risk.

Fair ball/foul ball: A legally hit ball that comes to rest or is touched between the third base line and the first base line is ruled a fair ball. If the ball hits one of the bases, it is a fair ball. If the ball bounds *over* first or third base and lands in *fair or foul* territory, it is also a fair ball. A ball that hits the plate is neither fair nor foul—yet. If, after hitting the plate, it is touched or comes to rest in fair territory (including on the plate), it is a fair ball; otherwise it is foul. A fly ball that is touched in the air in fair territory is a fair ball, even if after being touched it lands in foul ground. The ball is judged fair or foul by its position, not that of the fielder. In all of the above cases the *entire* ball does not have to be on or over fair territory to be considered fair. *Any* part of the ball and *any* part of the foul line are the determining factors.

Foul tip: A foul tip is a batted ball that goes from the bat (not higher than the batter's head) straight to the catcher's glove and is caught. In fast-pitch softball, there is an important distinction between foul tip and foul ball. A foul tip is live and the baserunners may be put out (e.g., an attempted steal may be in progress). If the ball is dropped, or if it first bounces off the catcher's chest protector or mask, it is a foul ball, and the ball is dead. In slow-pitch, a foul tip is always a dead ball.

Infield fly: An infield fly occurs with runners on first and second or bases loaded *and* less than two outs. It must be a *fair* fly ball that can be caught, with ordinary effort, by anyone stationed in the infield. Line drives or bunts in fast-pitch softball cannot be infield flies. The batter is automatically out (whether the ball is caught or not), and runners advance at their own risk. The umpire generally calls out "Infield fly! The batter is out!" when the fly reaches its peak. If your runners take off when the ball is hit, they can advance without penalty as long as the ball is not caught. If it is caught, though, they are liable to be doubled (or tripled) up.

Here is a common scenario in youth softball. With runners at first and second and no outs, an infield fly is declared. When the shortstop muffs the catch, the runners think they have to run, and do. Now the shortstop picks up the ball and throws it to the third baseman, who touches the bag for a forced out. No good. When the batter is out, the runners are not *forced* to advance. They *may* advance at their own risk and can be put out only by a *tag* play.

Intentional walk: In fast-pitch, the pitcher *must* throw four balls to the batter for an intentional walk. The pitches must be made because the ball is live and there is a possibility of a passed ball, wild pitch, illegal pitch, or a stolen base. In slow-pitch, where there is no advance on balls not hit, it makes no sense to throw the pitches for an intentional walk. The pitcher simply tells the umpire that he wants to intentionally walk the batter, and the batter is awarded first base. In co-ed play (in which male and female batters alternate in the batting order), the rules for slow-pitch apply, with one exception: If a male batter is walked, whether intentionally or not, the next batter, a female, has the option of taking a walk or hitting.

Interference: Interference occurs when a player on offense hinders a player on defense who is trying to make a play. Someone is always ruled out on an interference call. Teach your baserunners to avoid a fielder who is making a play. A baserunner may legally go in front of or behind a fielder. He *may not* stop or slow down in front of him so as to hinder his view. Umpires may call verbal interference. For example, a runner sprints by the shortstop, who is fielding a ground ball, yelling "Boot it! Boot it!" This is not only interference, it is unsportsmanlike and "bush league." Sometimes coaches are called for interference when they assist a baserunner rounding or returning to the bag (at first or third). Hands off, coach.

Obstruction: Obstruction occurs when a player on defense hinders a player on offense who is trying to hit the ball or run the bases. Most obstruction is committed by infielders getting in the way of baserunners. For example, after an extra base hit to right field, the first baseman, who is behind the bag, turns to the outfield to watch the play. This often places him directly in the baserunner's path. Since a baserunner's momentum generally takes him outside the diamond, teach your infielders to get inside to avoid him.

Catcher's obstruction occurs when the catcher's mitt contacts the bat during the hitter's swing. If the ball is not hit, a "dead ball" (a kind of time-out—no one can advance) results. The batter is awarded first base and all other runners stay on the base held at the time of the pitch, unless they are forced to advance because of the batter taking first. If the ball is hit, despite the obstruction, a "delayed dead ball" occurs. This means that the umpire will wait until the play is over before making a ruling. If the batter reaches first and all other runners advance at least one base, the play will stand. Otherwise, the umpire will give the offensive team manager the option of accepting the result of the play or having catcher's obstruction enforced (see above).

Out of the baseline: A runner is ruled out of the baseline when, in attempting to avoid a tag, he is more than 3 feet from a direct line to the next base. The baserunner is ruled out even without being tagged. A runner's momentum may take him well out of the normal basepath without his being called out. What defines his being out of the baseline is that a player with the ball attempts to tag him. Once the tag play awaits him, he can go no more than 3 feet to either side of a direct line to the base.

Overrunning first base: The baserunner may overrun first base and turn toward foul territory or second base without being tagged out. The direction of his turn does not put him in jeopardy. To be in jeopardy the baserunner *must make an attempt* to go to second base (in the umpire's judgment). This is actually an appeal play. The first baseman or other defender should verbalize, "Ump, he tried for second!" and tag him before he gets back to first. If the umpire rules that the runner did indeed attempt to go to second and then changed his mind, he will call him out.

We recommend that in this situation you teach your runner to walk nonchalantly back to first as if no attempt to second were made. If he sprints or dives back and doesn't make it in time, the umpire is liable to call him out because his action, in effect, tells the umpire that he made an attempt to second. No verbal appeal is necessary because both he and the defensive player are showing "by obvious action" that an appeal is being made.

Overthrows: An overthrow is a thrown ball that goes beyond the boundaries of the playing field into dead-ball territory. The ball is dead and the baserunners are awarded extra bases. All runners are awarded two bases from where they were *at the time the errant throw was released.* In fast-pitch, a pitch that goes out of play is ruled dead, and the baserunners are awarded one base.

Protests: A coach cannot protest a call based on the umpire's judgment. For example, he cannot protest balls and strikes, fair or foul balls, or safe or out calls. He *can* protest the umpire's misinterpretation of a rule or his giving an incorrect penalty on a play. He can also protest the umpire's applying the wrong rule to a play. All protests must be made to the plate umpire before the next pitch; the exception is a protest over player eligibility, which can be made even after a game is completed. Within a reasonable amount of time, usually 48 hours, a written protest must be filed with the area's umpire-in-chief. It must include date of game, umpires' names, and all essential facts on which the protest is based. The umpire-in-chief may rule that the protest is invalid, in which case the game is official. If the protest is upheld, however, the game will be replayed from the point of the incorrect decision, with the error corrected. Finally, if a protest about player eligibility is upheld, the game is forfeited to the protesting team.

Re-entry: *Any* starting player can leave the game and re-enter once, as long as he occupies the same spot in the batting order when he returns. The starting player and his substitute can never be in the line-up at the same time. For example, your shortstop can bat fifth and play for several innings. Then a substitute can go into the game for him. The substitute doesn't have to play short, but he does have to bat fifth. Later, the starting shortstop can return and must still bat fifth. The substitute must come out of the game and is no longer eligible to play. If the re-entry rule is violated, the manager and the player(s) involved are ejected from the game.

If you believe that your opponents are in violation of the re-entry rule, you must notify the home plate umpire in the form of a protest. It is different from other protests in that you may bring it to the umpire's attention at any time during the game, but everything that occurred while the illegal player was in the game will stand.

"Tie goes to the runner—he was safe, ump!": Forget it. Most good umpires will tell you that you must beat the ball to the bag if you want to be safe.

About the Authors

MARIO PAGNONI

Mario Pagnoni is a coach, a rules clinician, and a Massachusetts Amateur Softball Umpire-in-Chief. When not out on the softball field, he is a teacher in the public school system. Mario has written extensively for *The Boston Globe* and various computer magazines and has published several books as well. His first book, *The Complete Home Educator* (about teaching children at home with computers), was described by the late, noted educator John Holt as "...one of the best explanations I have ever seen of any scientific subject."

GERALD ROBINSON

Gerald Robinson, an English teacher and an active member of the local Amateur Softball Association board, has umpired softball for over fifteen years and has a thorough knowledge of the game. Gerald has also written for *The Boston Globe* and various computer magazines.

Credits
Book Production/Design: Mountain Lion, Inc.
Cover Design: Michael Bruner
Copyediting: Jean Atcheson
Photographs: John Mottern
Typesetting: Elizabeth Typesetting Company
Mechanical: Production Graphics
Cover Photograph: Focus on Sports Inc.